Shanelle Dawson lives in northern New South Wales, Australia, with her beloved wild-spirited daughter, Kialah. She has travelled extensively and lived in far too many places, though she's trying to rein in the adventure-seeker to grow more solid roots and foundations. Childcare has been a wonderful job throughout her life, among many other things, but she's intrigued to see how this next new chapter unfolds as she endeavours to transmute life's poison into good medicine for those in similar circumstances to her Mother. Just as her Mother, and her Mother's Mother before her, loved and delighted in swimming, so do Shanelle and Kialah. Dancing, singing to the Earth, meditation and good chocolate are the best of friends to navigate through this crazy and beautiful world. Shanelle has explored many healing modalities in her quest to come to peace with the tragic past and reunite with a sense of belonging in this world.

My Mother's Eyes

SHANELLE DAWSON

with Alley Pascoe

Note for Readers: This is a book that details a harrowing crime and the ongoing trauma that continues to impact. If you are distressed while reading the book, please see pages 285–289 for resources to help.

'Joy and Sorrow' from Kahlil Gibran's *The Prophet*, as reproduced on page 281, originally published in 1923 by Alfred A. Knopf, USA.

hachette
AUSTRALIA

Published in Australia and New Zealand in 2023
by Hachette Australia
(an imprint of Hachette Australia Pty Limited)
Gadigal Country, Level 17, 207 Kent Street, Sydney, NSW 2000
www.hachette.com.au

Hachette Australia acknowledges and pays our respects to the past, present and future Traditional Owners and Custodians of Country throughout Australia and recognises the continuation of cultural, spiritual and educational practices of Aboriginal and Torres Strait Islander peoples. Our head office is located on the lands of the Gadigal people of the Eora Nation.

A catalogue record for this work is available from the National Library of Australia

ISBN: 978 0 7336 5088 8 (paperback)

Cover, picture section and internal text design by Christabella Designs
Front cover and internal photographs courtesy of the author's family collection
Back cover photograph courtesy Emma Ní Rían
Typeset in 12.5/19pt Baskerville Regular by Kirby Jones
Printed and bound in Australia by McPherson's Printing Group

Dedicated to all Mothers and every Motherless child, everywhere

The deeper that sorrow carves into your being,
the more joy you can contain

—Kahlil Gibran, *The Prophet*

Contents

Foreword

The story of my Mother is one I need to tell, to reclaim. I am my Mother's daughter. I have been told I have my Mother's eyes and that when I was younger I strongly resembled her, though of course I've now outlived her by thirteen years. The wound of not having a mum has seeped into every aspect of my life. Sometimes the black hole she left behind vacuums me into its void, and the density of how she left us weighs heavily on my chest and shoulders, making it difficult to breathe.

Everyone has a story. This is mine. And hers. Our story.

You might have heard the story of my Mum, Lynette Joy Simms aka Dawson, or a version of it anyway. Part of her story has been written and reported about in the media, featured in the podcast *The Teacher's Pet*, on the television program *60 Minutes*, and investigated by the police. The story has been the basis of two coronial inquests, and a 2022 trial in the New South Wales Supreme Court where my father, Chris Dawson, was eventually found guilty of murdering my Mother and was sentenced to twenty-four years in prison.

The verdict came forty years, four months and one day after my Mum disappeared. My beautiful Mother left our lives on the 8th of January 1982. My younger sister, Sherry, was two and I was four. We grew up believing our Mum abandoned us. At the core of my being, I believe I've always known the truth of her disappearance, but it's taken many years of peeling back the lies and deceptive programming to come to see the tragic reality, the nightmare that lay at the foundation of my world, when life should have been kind, safe and carefree.

In these pages, I've capitalised Mum and Mother as a sign of respect. I haven't done the same for dad and father.

Some of you may find portions of this book completely unbelievable, unlike anything you've ever personally experienced … And some may find my journey tame compared to what you've lived to tell. My hope is that by sharing my story and by reaching out from my heart to yours, I may offer support, and encourage or inspire your own journey of life in some way.

Many of these pages are excerpts from my journals over the years, as well as dreams. I've been journalling from a young age and writing my dreams down since I was nineteen, always seeking messages from Spirit or, in later years, clues from my subconscious about what happened to my

Mother. I have had a lot of spiritual, ghost and otherworldly experiences throughout my life. These have been integral in defining who I am and how I perceive the world.

In these pages, I have shared entries of my internal struggle to try to comprehend the tragedy, raw and uncensored. Please don't judge me; have compassion and remember we're all just doing the best we can. My world has also been a beautiful tapestry of amazing people and life experiences, but woven through these moments in time has always been an underlying, compressed devastation just waiting for its time to be remembered, felt … and to be integrated back into its rightful place on my internal timeline.

It is my hope that by sharing this story, the lies told as truth may come out from their hiding place and that my Mother's life may be reclaimed from undeserved shame, to be honoured and cherished. Although we can't bring her back, we can try to save others from her fate. It is my hope that our tragedy might be a nudge to others in her situation, to recognise the red flags of domestic abuse and to know that we all deserve to have kindness and mutual respect in our relationships. I want you all to exist/exit safely; may that be my Mum's legacy.

May all wounds find the support they need to heal. May we get to the root of the problem and prevent the majority of this damage occurring in the first place. May we create systems in our society that support the healing of this epidemic of violence, in particular in what is supposed to be a sacred union. May the people who are harming also have the courage to ask for help and may it exist, thereby breaking the cycles of abuse. May the people who see harm speak up or offer support before it's too late. Domestic violence exists in a world where we turn a blind eye or don't know how to help, where we avoid asking the hard questions and pretend not to notice when a Mum-of-two vanishes into thin air. Or we shake our heads in momentary disgust as yet another fatality from domestic violence is reported on the news and yet we fail to do anything to change it. It's hard to know where to start. Abuse hides in the shadows, and it festers in silence. This desperately needs to change.

In breaking my silence, and by reaching out from my heart to yours, I hope you might feel less alone in your journey.

I write and dedicate this book to all of the people in the world who have known trauma and tragic heartbreak, in particular at the hands of someone they love. May our destructive pain find creative outlets to be transformed. May our nightmares find healing channels that bring to others, good medicine. May we all choose to act from a place of kindness as much as humanly possible. May all of the people who are selfishly destroying our planet, because of greed and misguided power, come to remember connection to Source, to the beauty of nature, hence to each other and themselves.

These are my memories, in truth as I remember them. Some names and details have been withheld or changed to protect privacy and to prevent litigation against me.

I write this book to honour my Mum and her life, taken from us for such selfish reasons, I can't even comprehend. I write this for my dear Nanna Simms who showed me love and integrity. And for my beautiful daughter, nieces and nephew and for the loving grandmother they will never know.

Ocean Lullabies and Invisible Arms
That Hold

As I sit on the Beach, my human senses long
To hear, feel, see and Know you
To feel your embrace holding me close
Your words of wisdom, your laughter
The speaking of my name in loving tones
And adoring your grandchildren
As a Grandmother should

The gravity of the ocean waves pull at my insecurities
Disolving uncertainty and reassuring me
Of what is known deep inside as solid truth.
That never were there any real
doubts of your love for me.
The salty kisses, ocean lullaby,
Soothes the space of longing for you
Reminding me you are still here

Though I miss your form your soul lives on
Your DNA sparks with life in your daughters' bodies
Now inherent in those of our children
I see you in the tenderness of our maternal instincts
in the graceful flutter of butterfly wings,
Hear you in the joy and sorrow of our hearts;
In the call of the sea, a whisper in a breeze
And feel your invisible arms that hold
us like the warmth of the sun.

Ancient whale songs speak to my bones
Of our maternal lineage of ancestral dreaming
A direct link to the stars where I see you shine
I love you, our beautiful Mother.

(I wrote this as a letter to my Mother
while I was living in Hervey Bay
on the 24th of August 2018.)

A Note from the Co-writer

My name is Alley Pascoe and I am a journalist and writer. Like so many Australians and people around the world I was captivated by the story of *The Teacher's Pet*, told prominently in an award-winning podcast by Hedley Thomas about the disappearance of Sydney woman Lynette Dawson in the 1980s, and the suspicion that her husband Chris had killed his wife. I listened to the podcast and read the news articles, and was saddened and shocked by the story that was unfolding. The story struck a nerve and it stayed with me, as I'm sure it did with many others. But that's what it was: a story. At the end of each episode and every news article, my life continued. Meanwhile, the lives of Lyn's loved ones continued to stand still. This wasn't a story to them; it was their lives.

In 2022, the story made headlines and caught my attention once again when Christopher Dawson stood trial for the murder of his wife. He was found guilty of the charge. I remember feeling relieved when I read the news. 'Yes, they got the bastard,' I thought to myself. Finally. For Lyn's family – including her eldest daughter Shanelle – the verdict was bittersweet. There were still so many questions, so much trauma, and more to the story. It was hearing Shanelle's victim impact statement that made me realise the story was far from over. When Shanelle addressed the court and her father, the raw emotion in her voice stabbed my heart. But the grace and strength of this woman blew me away. Shanelle was four years old when her mother was violently removed from her life. The ripples of that disappearance and murder would shape Shanelle's life from that moment on. In the courtroom that day, Shanelle showed such grit to stand before her father to tell him the cost of what he had done. And to ask him to reveal where her mother's body was. Imagine living with the knowledge that your father had murdered your mother and lied to you your whole life, allowing you to think she had left because she didn't love you anymore. What would that do to you? How could a father do this to his child? How could he do this to a woman he at one time loved?

It stopped me in my tracks. The sheer horror and tragedy of it all. I was so impressed with Shanelle Dawson on this day, honouring her mother and holding a mirror up to her father with such strength.

Then, earlier this year, I was asked if I would be interested in helping Shanelle Dawson write her story. I was honoured. Working with inspiring women, resilient women, has been one of the greatest gifts of my writing career. I jumped at the chance, and together Shanelle and I have talked for hours, as she allowed me into her world and told me about her life. While her life has been inextricably shaped by the loss of her mother, Shanelle is so much more than that. She is a poet, a creative soul, and a woman who in normal circumstances is capable of writing a book on her own. But these are not usual circumstances, and so she needed help to navigate the trauma she had lived through not as a therapist, but as a journalist telling a true story.

Helping someone write a book is a strange process as you take the truth and details of their lived experiences and help shape these into a narrative that readers can understand and connect with. Sometimes it means filling in gaps and giving information that the subject knows in their bones but still needs to be fleshed out for others to connect the threads. It means that my words and the subject's words can meld. Shanelle has then edited these words to make sure her story is not embellished or altered from her truth. There are places where I have added facts or recounted information gathered from court records and media reports. However, the text on these pages tells the truth of Shanelle's life. These are her words. Shanelle tells her story with truth and integrity, and shares parts of herself directly from her diary and dreams.

Together my hope is we allow you, the reader, to know her story and that it pays tribute to her mother, Lyn. I hope at the end you will all realise what a truly exceptional woman Shanelle Dawson is.

Preface

9th of July 2019
Lake Macquarie, New South Wales, Australia

I'm turning rocks over with my bare hands, hoping in my heart that I'll find what I need, what so many people need for closure. The truth. Justice. Answers to questions that have kept us awake and distraught for many a night; so many birthdays, anniversaries, too many years of wondering. I sit with journal in hand but this moment and the journey preceding it are much more intensely complicated and emotional than I can convey here in 2D words.

Today is my forty-second birthday and I'm here looking for my dear Mother's remains. It is not by design but by circumstance and convenience, a rare moment with family caring for my child for the day, so I could come on this quest. I could be celebrating with friends, or relaxing, but I'm in solemn determination and familiar grief instead. A wave of anger toward my father swells up; even though I'm choosing to be here looking, I feel compelled to, in order to reunite with my inner peace – something which his actions have temporarily stripped me of.

Earlier, I'd taken many a deep breath, my medicine drum ally by my side as I embarked in my car toward the Eraring Power Station. Two different psychics had given me matching descriptions of a potential location for finding my Mother's remains. They had both seen a jawbone under rocks, alongside a river or stream and among trees. That was enough for me to act on their visions. I know it seems impossible to most, but I do believe miracles can occur and I did feel that my Mother's invisible presence was guiding me every step of the way, as were the ancestors of the lands, to whom I paid my respects and asked permission of. The legal system is a lengthy and complicated process requiring massive patience, which at this time I didn't have. So I set out, if only for my actions to bring me comfort that at least I've tried in a way that makes plausible sense to me and helps me feel more empowered in an extremely helpless situation.

The descriptions from both psychics were of particular landmarks and in a general location. I parked my car and walked in the direction I felt inexplicably drawn to, my surroundings feeling oddly familiar as though I'd seen them in a dream. Firstly, I walked along a grassy, narrow

14

path and out onto the road, where I skirted along the fenced boundaries of the coal plant. I felt to turn left down a street and found myself passing a playing field, which was one of the landmarks foreseen by one of the psychics. I encountered a stream running alongside some fenced-off areas.

Regular déjà vu feelings and goosebumps intrigued me and as I scanned the scene before me, I asked my Mother to show me the way. I crossed a metal grated bridge over the flow of water coming in from Lake Macquarie and here it intersects with the toxic run-off from the power plant.

Later there will be people fishing off another bridge further down the stream, but for now I am alone. I find some rocks to sit on with the salt marsh mangroves behind me and the two towers of the coal plant looming on a near horizon, their industrial harshness in stark contrast to the gentle, natural beauty before me.

I sing a song on my drum. Many a time when I've not wanted to exist in such a difficult place, my drum has kept me connected to the Earth. It brings me back to my body and helps clear away the blockages. I know it may seem strange to some, but many Indigenous cultures worldwide know the medicine of the drum and I've moved through massive things without drugs, alcohol or TV to numb my pain and my drum has helped with that.

I sing a song. Author unknown.

Earth Mother, we honour your body
Earth Mother, we honour your bones
Earth Mother, we enter your body
Earth Mother, we sing to your stones
Awey awey awey oh away away away oh aha
Awey awey awey oh.

After my song, I received a visit from a security guard. I wasn't in any way trespassing but I understand I would have looked quite strange sitting there on the rocks … and how do I explain what I'm doing there?! I decided not to! He expressed his concern that I might go for a swim; I reassured him that I had no intention of doing that and he left me to it. I called both of the psychics at different stages, who were kindly giving of their time for free. I found some white feathers on the path alongside the stream, which are often a sign to me that Spirit, my Mother or angelic presences are near. I was on a video call with one of the psychics and pointed the camera toward a spot by a tree among the mangroves, where I felt magnetically stuck to and she began to cry.

CHAPTER ONE

Vanished into Thick Air

Sadly, I don't really remember my beautiful Mother. Perhaps that's due to trauma or my young age – I was only four and a half and my sister was two and a half years old at the time she was murdered – or because at the time, the main people around us didn't help to keep her memory alive. When we would visit our dear Nanna Simms, Mum's mother, she would share photos and stories, but with such deep sadness that I didn't fully understand the extent of until I grew older. I always believed and assumed that we'd find Mum, or she'd return. So, her absence wasn't yet permanent in my heart.

While I don't have clear memories of my Mum, I have a few precious snippets about her, like the oat scrub bag she left on the side of the bath, and the antique, black frosted-glass mirror, which used to hang in her bathroom, and features a voluptuous lady's bum, visible as she steps into a metal tub.

I don't have real-life, animated memories of her, but I have her smile and the love in her eyes etched accessibly in my mind from many hours of gazing at photos of her, longingly devouring every detail, every beautiful little line that appears next to her eyes when she smiles ... As though that might somehow bring her back, or bring me clues as to what happened. When I was little, there were no photos of Mum around except for a very few which were kept in a shoebox alongside a lock of my baby hair, up high and shoved to the back of the cupboard. I cherished those tiny remnants of my Mum so much, though I certainly never pulled them out to look at them when my father was around, or often at all.

Growing up without my Mother was as though I had a deep and huge, gashing wound that nobody but her knew how to tend to. Nobody else in the immediate family acknowledged her and we didn't discuss her, so she became the elephant in the room. If anybody in the outer circle of family ever mentioned my Mum, there was an uncomfortable silence; obviously they weren't aware of the unwritten code. Pretending somebody never existed doesn't make it so.

My Mother was born on the 25th of September 1948, in Sydney, Australia, to parents Helena and Len Simms. She grew up in Clovelly in the Eastern Suburbs, with her brothers Greg and Phil, and her big sister Pat, with whom she was particularly close.

The four Simms kids had sun-bleached blonde hair and sun-kissed tanned skin. They used to walk from Clovelly to

South Coogee and swim or practise their laps in the ocean pool, just down the hill from their house. Pat tells how when they were very little 'we'd go around to a place called the Bogey Hole, which was behind Clovelly. And there was always a watchful mother [my Nanna Simms] sitting above making sure that everything was okay. There was a pool there and that was quite magical when we were small.' I'm fairly certain my Mother and her siblings spent more time in the water than out. They'd swim all year long, in the middle of winter and the thick of summer. They would collect sticks for bonfire night and set off crackers. The older sisters would dress the little brothers up in make-up. It sounds like it was a great childhood.

There's a story about my Mum in her youth that captures her spirit. Her high school had a strict uniform policy with gloves and a hat. Within days of starting at the school, Mum's hat got blown off her head and landed in the path of a double-decker bus. The bus ran straight over the hat, and for the rest of her schooling, she had tyre marks across her hat. That was Mum, she was her own person. Mum was bright, sparky and self-confident. She called a spade a spade and she always stood up for what she believed in.

As an adult, my Mother had golden hair, an easy smile and warm eyes. I have my Mother's eyes, so I'm told.

Pat describes Mum as being 'just a lovely, lovely person'. She says my Mother was 'gentle and caring, calm, funny.' And that she was always the 'first one to ring for birthdays.

If she could give one gift, she'd give three ... she was just so generous.'

Greg remembers her similarly as a 'happy, gentle, generous and loving daughter, sister, mother, niece, aunt and friend'.

My father, Christopher Michael Dawson, was born on the 26th of July 1948, also in Sydney. His mum and dad were Joan and Sydney (Skeet) Dawson. Dad grew up in Maroubra, with his identical twin brother Paul, his older brothers Peter and Gary and sister, Lynelle. Dad and Paul weren't just close, they were inseparable; they had their own secret language that only they and their mother could understand, and they had to do speech therapy to learn to speak properly. They got a lot of attention being twins, and I get the sense that they were quite mollycoddled. They also loved the fact they were dressed the same throughout childhood and often as adults would show up wearing the same thing unintentionally. At some point as kids they trialled being placed in different classes at school. This was because the school thought they were cheating, because their answers were always the same. Apparently, their answers remained the same and they were both miserable being separated and were returned to the same class. I believe they were bullied a bit in their younger years and I wonder how that affected them psychologically and their future choices in life. Their mum certainly doted on them – she called them her twinnies – and from what I can tell, was very involved in their lives, certainly watching every game of football from the sidelines like a hawk. It felt like they were the favourites. Dad and Paul definitely worked the twin thing; as young men they both played for the Newtown Jets then went on to become PE teachers. They were mirror images of each other and once shared a job, washing dishes as though they were one person. One of them even sat in for the other's driving test, so his brother wouldn't miss playing a football game.

Mum and dad were both prefects at high school, Sydney Girls High School and Sydney Boys High School respectively. They met at a school dance in 1965 when they were both sixteen. Five years later, they were married at St Jude's Church in Randwick. Paul was dad's best man, and my Mum chose Auntie Pat as one of her bridesmaids. She looked every bit the beautiful, glowing bride. Together, in their wedding photos, Mum and dad appeared to be very much in love and joyous. One of my favourite photos is of my Mother putting her wedding garter on my dad's leg; she looks blissfully happy and I love that this depicts her cheeky side (which I may have inherited).

Together, Mum and dad were good-looking, well-dressed and respected. They didn't smoke, my Mother drank minimally and my father, not at all. They were a golden couple of sorts. There's footage of them together from 1975, when they appeared on an ABC TV show about twins called *Chequerboard*, alongside dad's brother Paul. In the video, which is hard for me to watch, Mum looks confident, calm, and endearingly committed to my father. She gazes at him lovingly as she talks about the unusually close bond the twin brothers share. Mum has an air of grace around her. Stumbling on that footage was like finding pure gold.

After my parents got married, when Mum and dad bought land on the Northern Beaches of Sydney in Bayview, Paul and his wife, Marilyn, bought the block two doors down. Both dad and Paul lived on the same street and worked as teachers at Cromer High School. Mum trained as a nurse at the Royal Alexandra Children's Hospital in Camperdown. There's a photo of her at work kneeling beside a young patient's bedside. My auntie told me that the photo was actually taken on Mum's day off; that she'd gone into work to check on her patient. That's the kind of woman she was. After graduating and working as a nurse, she was later hired to work as a registered nurse in an early childhood centre, as was a requirement in those days.

I know my Mum completely adored my dad and they enjoyed a great social and active life together with regular tennis games and parties. Both Mum and dad really wanted to be parents. They tried to conceive for six or seven years, but she was told she was unable to, due to blocked fallopian tubes. She underwent surgery in a last attempt to fall pregnant, had almost given up and was looking into adoption, when she found out she was pregnant with me. There's a photo of Mum at her brother Greg's wedding when she would have been one-month pregnant with me. I wonder if she knew she was pregnant yet?

I only know the details of my birth from my father's perspective and from what's on my birth certificate. I was born on the 9th of July 1977 at Crown Street Hospital in Sydney. I know I was born via caesarean and that the nurse brought me out to my father who was in the waiting room. The nurse was apparently reluctant to pass me over as she was enjoying cuddling me. My father's version of my birth story never included much about my Mother. I don't know if she cried when I finally appeared, how she recovered, if she sang to me … I don't know because my Mum never got the chance to tell me about it. My birth story is yet another thing I've lost to the black hole left by the absence of my Mother.

Two years and two days after I was born, Mum welcomed my sister Sherry to the world. We were her girls, her world, I'm told. I always thought our father and uncle would've preferred boys, so they could teach them football in their footsteps. My father denies this, but I find it curious that both he and Paul went on to have three daughters each, no sons.

Our brown, brick house in Bayview was at the top of a short but steep driveway and surrounded by native bushland and sclerophyll forest. There was a paved veranda out the front, then some stairs down to the lush pool area and a trampoline in the bushy backyard. Further up the sloped yard, the neighbours behind us had a deer enclosure.

At the bottom of our driveway, down near the road, there was a cluster of large boulders that seemed massive to me as a little girl. I can remember spending quite a lot of time down there, climbing over the rocks and playing make-believe with my sister.

It was a beautiful house and I've been told how much my Mother loved it. She had a good eye for detail and an earthy flair and lovingly decorated our house with rugs, pictures, baskets and shells, to make it a nurturing home. I want to believe it started out as a happy and nourishing home, before it turned into a hellish nightmare.

There are things I've heard as an adult about my parents' relationship: about the bruises, the fights, the infidelity. I'm reported to have witnessed those things, though I was certainly oblivious to it all until I read the police statements in more recent years.

My mother didn't drive. She never learned how to since neither of her parents drove and she grew up within walking distance of public transport. In Bayview, we lived on a street without a bus line, in a suburb where public transport was scarce. When Mum went to work or wanted to go somewhere, she would have to ask dad, or Paul and Marilyn, or walk. I can imagine Mum taking Sherry and I for lots of walks around the bottlebrush-scented streets of Bayview, but I don't have any actual memories of her doing so.

I can look back on my Mum's inability to drive and see it for what it was: a control tactic. Mum was essentially trapped at home. She was dependent on my father and in-laws to access life outside of our street. Why did they choose to live somewhere without public transport knowing my Mother couldn't drive? Why didn't my father teach her?

Out of all the things I've been told about my Mum, this is what I've heard the most: my Mum was a beautiful-hearted, kind and nurturing Mum who loved and doted on both me and my sister … And later, that she would never have abandoned 'her girls' of her own accord. That had she left, she would've taken us with her. I did come to believe she would not have left us girls, or the home she loved, willingly. It wasn't until I was a grown woman that I would hear testimonies from her friends.

Annette Leary, a woman she worked with at the childcare centre said, 'She was such a good mother. She was so proud of [Shanelle and Sherry] as well … she loved them.'

Another friend of hers from work, Susan Strath, said Mum used to talk about us all the time: 'She loved them dearly … she was very excited because the eldest one, she was getting ready for her to go to school … She had a great relationship with them. She was a great Mum.'

Julie Andrew, who was my Mother's neighbour at Bayview, said 'She was an Earth Mother. Nothing would come between her and her kids.'

And Roslyn McLoughlin, who Mum played tennis with, said: 'She absolutely adored them. They were the light … she really doted on her children and loved them very much and they were her priority in her life.'

My father rewrote our history by telling us our Mother didn't love us. I only wish I had heard these words about my Mum when I was growing up. But my father controlled the narrative and so my Mother and her friends were erased from my life. And everything changed.

I have no clear memories of the last time I saw my Mum or the night she 'left', just the nightmarish ones that reappeared in more recent years. I've subconsciously blocked memories out to protect myself in order to survive, to function and to stay living all of these years with my father without completely losing it! Trauma, as we know, can affect long-term memory and recall, though certain things such as sounds or smells associated with those painful moments can trigger fragments of those memories.

I believe those memories are still stored inside of me, frequently blocking my clear sight, my foresight, hindsight and insight. I have tried through various means to access them. It's extremely frustrating that they remain elusive and yet their reverberations lurk in the shadows, affecting my physical and mental health. Snippets of memories have flashed in my mind throughout the decades, and I've never understood why they were so abstract or why they never stuck around long enough with additional detail for me to make sense of them. I've tried to grasp them, to reclaim them and to see the next sequence. One day I will reach the full memories where they hide and release their shackles, once and for all, in order to feel completely free again.

A Memory

Our front door. My teddy bear outside. It's raining. The driveway. 'I want My Mummy!!! Where is she?' An unfamiliar babysitter pulls me away from the door. I don't want to move. A tantrum. 'I WANT MY MUMMY!' I feel distressed and angry at this female for keeping me from my ... teddy.

The day after my Mother vanished was the 9th of January 1982. Mum was meant to take Sherry and I to the Northbridge Baths to meet Nanna Simms and Phil Day (my father's friend and other best man at his wedding) for a swim. My dad worked part-time at the Baths as a lifeguard. Mum had told her mother the plan for the day over a phone call, the night before. It was the last time Nanna Simms heard her daughter's voice and she recorded in her diary that she'd sounded 'sozzled', which was unusual given that my Mother wasn't a big drinker.

Nanna had been worried about Mum. She knew things hadn't been good between my Mother and father, and that they'd been fighting. Dad hadn't spent Christmas or New Year's Eve with us. In a letter dated 4th of January 1982, Nanna wrote to her other daughter, Pat, who lived on a property without any phone reception. Part of the letter read …

So with all the stress and strain on Lyn, it sure is telling in her face.

Saddest Christmas I've had.

Lyn wants Chris to go see the doctor … to see what is making him so angry with her.

I wonder if Nanna Simms was surprised when dad brought us to the Northbridge Baths instead of Mum, who was nowhere to be seen. I'm sure we would have been perplexed at why Mum wasn't there with us. It was unlike her. She was reliable and dearly loved her mother; she would never willingly miss a gathering of loved ones.

According to my father, he received an 'unexpected' phone call from Mum while we were at the pool. He claims she told him she needed some time away and was going to the Central Coast with some friends. I don't remember seeing dad take the call and there were no witnesses to it.

I do remember a conversation between dad and Nanna Simms at the pool where what he was saying wasn't as I knew it to be. I can't remember what he was saying now; I assume it was the part where he dropped her at the bus stop in the early morning. I wish I could remember the details – but whatever it was, it was wrong. Confused as to why he was lying, I tried to correct dad's version of events. He grabbed my arm firmly and grimaced through gritted teeth as he led me to a spot next to the entrance of the pool, near the turnstiles.

I could tell I was in trouble, though I didn't know why … I hadn't done anything wrong! There were too many people coming through the entrance on a hot summer's day, so he led me into the bathrooms instead. I was conscious of whether anyone could overhear us from the stalls and felt a sense of shame at being scolded. I also vividly recall the indignant outrage and stubborn anchoring in my legs I felt – and still to this day carry – but I can't remember what he threatened me with. Whatever it was, it was enough to shut me up for the next thirty-seven years. And whatever it was that I witnessed from that fateful previous night faded into a distant nightmare, inaccessible to my conscious mind.

A Poem

2018
Hervey Bay, Queensland

Mother

I don't know how to relate to the concept of Mother
Where that solid form of comfort should be is just air
Space that has longed to be filled for so long
But how to fill a space worthy of nothing less than Mother
Mother Earth has done her best
I feel her under my feet and flowing through every
beat of my heart and all of the space in between
She has held me well
As has the air I breathe into every cell of my
being, every fibre that's known to me
But a massive gaping, gasping black hole still exists
Where a Mother should be
All I can do is breathe and cry into where I long for her

CHAPTER TWO

Raised by a Child

My babysitter turned stepmother didn't wear white to her wedding. She wore a peach-coloured dress with pleats. It was the early eighties and a lot of fashion was hideous then. I don't remember the dress, but I've seen it in photos. Nor do I remember the wedding, but I know I was there because there's a photo of me in my cheap flower girl outfit standing on the steps, alongside my sister and cousins. My stepmother, who I'll call J in these pages, was a young bride. She had been one of my father's PE students at Cromer High School and was brought into our lives as a babysitter when she was sixteen. She was the cool teenager who looked after my sister and me when our parents went out.

In late 1981, J came to stay with us – my Mother, father, sister and me – in Bayview. J had told our dad about her difficult home life. She lived in an apartment in nearby Dee Why with her mother and violent stepfather. It was an extremely damaging and unsafe home situation and I have compassion for her because of this, as would've my Mother because she was a kind-hearted person. My father would've suggested it wasn't the best place for someone doing their Year 12 exams – which J was – so he invited her to live with us. Looking back now, I wish J had just gone to live with her father or one of her older sisters. There were other options, but apparently she claimed they were too disruptive to her life, too far from her friends and school – so she disrupted our lives instead and moved in with us. I wonder how my Mother felt about that, or if she even felt she had a choice? Mum handled it with as much grace as she could. J has said she saw my Mum as a mother figure and that Mum took care of her like a mother would.

Then one day, J went from being our occasional babysitter to our live-in babysitter, at least that's what people were told. But what they didn't know was that at Christmas, dad gave her a card that read: 'Happy Christmas. Once or twice every minute. Love always. God.' When J was asked why dad had signed the card as 'God' she said it was because he wanted to disguise who he was because it was 1980, she was sixteen, and that's what he called himself. It's repulsive.

Two months later, when J turned seventeen, dad gave her a card that said: 'Happy 17th birthday my little chickadee.'

'To my lovely, beautiful bub,' he wrote in it. 'Hoping today is a very happy one and knowing we will share all the birthdays to follow. All my love forever xxx.'

I remember enjoying having J as our babysitter and I'm sure our father's enthusiasm for her would've influenced that as well. One afternoon in late 1981, when J was still just the babysitter, my sister and I walked up the road to Paul and Marilyn's house to see our cousins. When we got there, our cousins wouldn't let us come in. They were being very mysterious, and I remember one of the cousins secretly admitting that J was inside. I recall feeling jealous that she was there with them and not staying with us anymore. I'm assuming that might've been when she left our house to move in with Paul and Marilyn for a short stint, just before she went to South West Rocks for an end of Year Twelve celebration at the very start of 1982.

I don't know why J moved in with my uncle and auntie. Again, I wonder if Marilyn had any objections to the teenager moving into her home, or if she too felt an obligation to go along with what the twins wanted?

According to evidence, this is what happened ...

J says my Mum confronted her, allegedly saying: 'You've been taking liberties with my husband.' There were signs, even though I'm sure my Mother wouldn't have wanted to see them. When my Mum wasn't home, J apparently used to walk around our pool topless and in a G-string. She said dad didn't call Mum 'Lyn', he called her fatso. She also claims dad used to mix Valium into an alcoholic drink for Mum and wait for her to fall asleep, so they could have sex under the same roof as my Mother, while she was there passed out. The utter disrespect and selfishness makes me want to vomit. How dare he dishonour her like that? His actions trigger such massive rage in me.

J claims she didn't say anything to my Mother when she confronted her in this way. I don't believe that she didn't respond in any way and I wonder if there's more to the story there …

These aren't things that I remember myself; they're details I've learned from police statements, court proceedings and news articles, but having seen glimpses of my father's 'other' side over the years, I can imagine him doing that.

A few days before Christmas in 1981, J says she bundled her things into garbage bags and threw them in the back of dad's car, where he'd packed his clothes and pillow, so they could set off to start a new life together in Queensland. Before they hit the road, dad left a note for Mum saying, 'Don't paint too dark a picture of me to the girls.' They didn't even make it to the Queensland border before J supposedly got homesick and made dad turn around. J and dad arrived back in Sydney on Christmas Day, 1981, but dad didn't come home to spend the day with his wife and children. I've heard that he hid out with J at Paul and Marilyn's house, and that they later went to Forest High School, where Paul was a teacher, to sleep in the school gym.

I don't know if Mum tried to hide dad's absence at Christmas from us, or if we were oblivious to the entire situation. Did we ask where our daddy was when we sat down to open our Christmas presents? Did we look for him around the table at Christmas lunch? Seems to me, he certainly had his priorities fucked up! But, that's what obsession does.

In January, J went on a holiday to South West Rocks with two of her sisters and some friends as an end-of-year celebration. She was there when my Mother 'disappeared'. Dad reportedly called to tell her, 'Lyn's gone. She's not coming back. Come back to Sydney and help me look after the children and be with me.' The next day, according to witness statements, dad drove the five hours to South West Rocks to pick her up and bring her back to Bayview.

It is debated as to when exactly J moved into our family home permanently, after my Mother disappeared, though I suspect it was immediately. Even though my father would've been on school holidays, I can't imagine him being able to juggle his two children, house chores, provide meals (he didn't cook), and the odd jobs he picked up. Of course, there's also the fact that he was obsessed with J and would want the object of his fixation to be near as soon as possible, pretending to play happy family as though my beautiful Mother never existed.

It took dad six weeks to report our Mother missing. On the 18th of February 1982, he went to Mona Vale police station to file a missing person's report; Nanna Simms had begged him to do so. Dad told the police the last time he saw Mum was on the morning of the 9th of January 1982 when he dropped her off at the bus stop to go to the shops. He said he'd heard from her several times by phone since then and that there was no concern for her welfare.

The local police on the Northern Beaches – some of whom played football with my father and his brother – filed the case away as a runaway wife.

More than a month after finally reporting Mum missing, dad placed an ad in the *Daily Telegraph* newspaper. 'Lyn, I love you, we all miss you. Please ring. We want you home. Chris,' it read.

While dad was playing the abandoned husband publicly, privately he was settling in with J.

There were rumours. After my Mother disappeared, dad was quietly transferred from Cromer High (where he'd taught J) to Beacon Hill High. There'd been talk between students and teachers at his old school that he and J were 'in love'. When J moved into our family home and started wearing my Mother's clothes, the talk couldn't be ignored. Other disturbing and worrying things were said as well. It seemed to be common knowledge that teachers from Cromer High, including my dad, would go to the Time and Tide Hotel near the school and buy alcohol for their underage students. Reports have since been published that a number of teachers from schools on the Northern Beaches used their positions of power to lure adolescents into bed. It was inappropriate, predatory – and covered up. The sexual misconduct was an open secret. Instead of addressing the fact that my dad had shacked up with his student, the school just moved him along. Just like they do with the Catholic priests who are paedophiles. Out of sight, out of mind.

Nanna Simms always said how much she loved waking up to the birdsong when she'd stay in our spare room at Bayview. My sister and I encouraged her to come and stay with us again soon, to which she replied, 'Oh, J will be in the spare room, so there won't be enough room for me.'

'No, J stays in dad's bed,' my sister innocently stated.

I remember my father saying he and J would get married but had to wait for her to turn eighteen.

When our Mother went 'missing', we had no idea what was going on. One day our Mum was there, the next she wasn't. Our dad told us Mum had left because she didn't love us anymore. It was a viciously cruel thing to say to us, although I don't consciously remember my father saying the words out loud. It's difficult to measure how damaging that sentiment would have been to my young psyche. The abandonment issues ran deep within me.

There was an undercurrent of adult conversations that we weren't privy to. I would have been confused that it was now J picking us up from school, not our Mother with our dad. She just slotted right in, didn't she?!

Seven months after Mum disappeared, dad applied for a divorce. He got a court order for the dissolution of his marriage to our Mother on the basis of abandonment. He claimed to be a 'forlorn, abandoned husband'. The divorce was granted and dad was awarded all marital assets –

including our home in Bayview – and custody of my sister and I. The divorce made way for a new marriage.

A year after my Mother ceased to exist, J and my dad married at our home in Bayview on the 15th of January 1984. I find it curious that for a supposedly close family, there were very few Dawsons at the wedding. It makes me wonder if they possibly didn't approve. Or if any of them knew, or suspected, the truth about what had happened to my Mother.

J was now adorned in my Mother's wedding rings, as well as her clothes. Surely, my Mother would've been wearing her rings? Why would she have taken them off? My father told my grandmother that Mum still had her rings, so Nanna Simms held onto the reassurance that Mum could always sell her rings if she needed money. Yet another lie my father shovelled.

Did it not occur to my father to keep them to give to my sister and I? It has been suggested I reclaim them back from J's daughter who apparently has them, but I don't want them. What they represent to me is no longer purity, trust, love, commitment but instead selfish betrayal, brutal dishonouring and doom.

At some point, we started calling J 'Mum'. We are quoted by our Nanna Simms as saying some horrible, brainwashed things, such as: Mummy wasn't our real Mother, J's our Mother now.

That must have been a dagger to Nanna Simms' heart. Not only had her daughter been taken away, now the memory of her daughter and all respect owed to her was being erased.

On a cold winter's day in July, Nanna Simms came to our primary school to bring my sister and I birthday presents and J wouldn't let her talk to or see us for some reason. We didn't understand why our beloved Nanna had suddenly become an enemy and I'll never comprehend why on earth my father and J (obviously under my father's instructions) treated her as such. My beautiful Nanna, she endured so much heartache and certainly did nothing to deserve this abuse.

When J hauled us away from our grandmother, I heard Nanna call J a 'slut'. As we drove away, I remember asking J what a slut was, but there was no reply. I know my Nanna never spoke like that and that she prided herself on being a 'lady', so she must've been extremely upset to say such a word, especially in front of her grandchildren. It breaks my heart.

I remember getting into trouble at kindy and then school around this time for being 'naughty', for biting, hitting and kicking other children. Paul's youngest daughter and I were dubbed 'Salt and Pepper' because we were always getting into conflict together, as well as for our blonde and fair versus olive and brunette complexions. I can understand now, though, the effect that trauma has and that it was the only way I had to communicate my big feelings at the time.

I'm not sure exactly when J's attitude toward us changed – whether it was when she went from babysitter to stepmother almost overnight or if it was more gradual. I know she says things changed for her once she had her own child, but I believe she started treating us more distantly before that. We were still in Sydney – before K was born – when we were told we had to call our father 'dad' now, not 'daddy', and that J was no longer to be called 'mummy', but was to be called by her name.

J is on record talking about her feelings toward us and our father's expectations of her. 'He always wanted me to love his two children like my own … and I just couldn't,' J has said. 'He wanted us to be just a happy little family … If I reprimanded the two older girls, he'd get stuck into me. So, of course, I had no control over them so I couldn't see us being a happy little family like he wanted.'

I felt unloved by J. She didn't want to be my mother and she certainly wasn't. I don't agree with her saying she had no control over us, though; I remember her having complete control of me and my sister. As I've said, she was the regulator and enforcer of the rules over us.

In moments when I casually relayed some of J's treatment toward us to Marilyn and Paul, I remember them exchanging looks. They weren't the only ones with raised eyebrows. One of J's friends said these words about the 'harsh' treatment we were subjected to when interviewed on the podcast investigating my Mother's disappearance.

'I know that she [J] wasn't very nice to his children, and I felt badly for them because they were quite young and I thought it's not their fault,' the friend said. 'There was no love. She didn't *like* them. She was really awful to them. She did what she had to for them, but it seemed like she didn't really want to spend any time with them.'

Years later, both her father and her sister stated they had concerns about the way J treated my sister and me at times. Confusingly, I also remember feeling protective toward J, perhaps in the same way a mistreated dog still feels loyal to its owner.

Despite all the traumatic things that were going on during this time, it was all downplayed to us kids. I have happy memories of staying with Nandi and Pop, dad's parents, and most of the cousins at their holiday house at Shoalhaven, which is about 200 kilometres south of Sydney. Adventuring across sand dunes playing cowboys and Indians, mucking around on blow-up boats and pulling cheeky, harmless tricks on each other. Our Pop volunteered himself to be in charge of the kid entertainment; he adored us all and was like a big, playful child himself. We each had a nickname and he'd sing silly little songs to us. We'd put on performances for Nandi and Pop and they'd have to sit through the shows and clap for us.

Once I was at university, I remember enjoying one-on-one visits with my Nandi as well. Previously I had only had time with her and Pop with other people around, so it was special to have quality time with her. Nandi told me of her mother's mother, who read tea leaves. She told me about Florence Nightingale being our distant cousin, and she spoke about my Mother. I listened intently as Nandi told me of a time when she was in significant discomfort and my Mother had accompanied her to the hospital (I'm assuming my Pop had driven, as my Nandi didn't drive either). They had placed her in the waiting room in the hospital and seeing her mother-in-law's pain, my Mum had insisted on speaking to the doctor on duty and demanded he saw her right away. Nandi credits my Mother for saving her life that day (I believe it was a burst appendix).

There's this misconception that women in abusive relationships are weak. My Mother may have spoken softly at times, but her voice and spirit were also strong and determined. I've been told it was also my Mother who stood up to her own father, when he was being a 'bit of a bully' toward her mother.

It was only a few months after getting married that J became pregnant and, around this time, we packed up and moved to Queensland, along with Paul and his family, and our Nandi and Pop Dawson. It must've been very difficult for them to leave their other children and grandchildren behind. But as it was when they were kids, the 'twinnies' came first. Where Chris and Paul went, Nandi and Pop followed.

While my father kept his parents close, he shut Nanna Simms out. He didn't even tell her we were moving to Queensland, she found out through family friends. My poor Nanna, it must have been heartbreaking for her, yet again.

In my memories of this time, J looks sour and unhappy, but for photos her scowl was dropped. I have photos of our drive to Queensland, though I don't remember it. Most photos show us all with our arms by our sides, though any feigned smiles from J, in posed photos taken over the years, was not carried on beyond that moment. I felt no love, warmth or kindness directed at me from the woman who wore my Mother's weddings rings.

When we first arrived in Queensland, we rented a house in Helensvale on the Gold Coast for six months while our house at Coomera was being built. We were excited to learn that at our new Queensland school, we were allowed to wear sandals. At home, things were less free.

Life was ruled by order, control and fear. Everything had its place, and you didn't dare move things. There were no toys in the living room; they were strictly kept in our bedroom/s. During the week, we weren't allowed out of our room/s until after 7 am (unless we needed to use the bathroom), and on weekends, it was 8 am. Everything we did in the house was highly regulated and enforced by J. When we brushed our teeth or washed our hands, we had to wipe the water off the basin, so it was completely dry. I had to stay completely still while I was having my hair brushed or there would be a consequence.

Food was tightly controlled. We had to eat everything we were given and we couldn't ask for more. I remember being locked in the laundry back in Bayview for not eating my dinner. We were taught to politely decline food if we were offered any at someone else's house.

My sister and I weren't allowed to roam and play freely around the house; we played only in our rooms or outside. On weekends, we were pushed out of the house. Sometimes we'd be dropped off at our 'babysitter' – the theme park Dreamworld – and left there all day. It might seem spoilt and ungrateful, but we would get bored. We'd have to stand out the front on our own and wait to be picked up. We were left at home alone when J and dad went grocery shopping, and we'd raid the Coco Pops, peanut butter, Vitamin C and fluoride tablets. We became masters at not taking too much and putting things back exactly like they were because we were afraid of J finding out.

My sister and I spent a lot of time together, and we were trauma bonded, so we were close in that regard. Our play fights almost always turned to real ones, though we'd hide the fact from 'the parents', bribing each other so we wouldn't get in trouble.

I recall a moment at our primary school after a school camp, looking for one of my lost items with J in the lost property and running into my teacher at the time. Mrs Jessop relayed to J that we all 'had a wonderful time at camp, swapping clothes and …'. I didn't hear the rest; I froze as I knew I wasn't allowed to do that and I'd be getting into trouble for it.

Sherry and I were good kids; we did well at school and in sport. We were polite and obedient. Every week, we did our paid chores: weeding the pavement and top garden, as well as doing dishes, emptying the dishwasher, helping carry in the groceries, keeping our rooms immaculate. We were not 'princesses', as J claims, we were kids who didn't deserve to feel separate from our dad and our sister, and to feel so isolated in our own home. We were kids who had lost our Mum, but we felt little kindness from J.

A Dream

12th of October 2010
La Gomera, Canary Islands, Spain

My sister has fallen into the toilet and is covered in poo. She's only little. I help her toward the shower and clean her up by tipping the toilet upside down.

I look in the mirror and am shocked to see the right side of my face is darkly bruised.

Am I my Mother?

I wish I could write about happy days with a shitty child mother replacement. Perhaps the happy memories are there, but what I remember is harsh coldness and constantly walking on eggshells because I felt we were always getting undeservedly into trouble for something. In contrast, our father was loving and kind toward us and would stand up for us. J acted differently towards us when he was around, so ironically in those years, he took on a hero archetype in my perception.

When our half-sister was born, to my mind, things became even more fractured. The arrival of J's daughter pushed me further away. It was the three of them and the two of us. On the night our new sister was born, Sherry and I went to stay with Paul, Marilyn and our three cousins at their house. K was born on the 8th of January 1986. Of course, I didn't realise the significance of that date at the time. My half-sister was born exactly four years to the day after my Mum 'disappeared'!

—

Our brick house in Coomera was large and decorated similarly to how my Mother had styled our Bayview home, and with many of the same items, though there was an emptiness that couldn't be filled. The property was seven and a half acres, and initially we were the only house in the street with very few houses for miles. Paul and his family were up the road in the next street, on ten acres with a similar house, pool and tennis court. Both Dawson brothers had sprawling houses, dalmatians from the same litter, and three girls each. Our families were mirror images of each other, except our Mother had been 'replaced' with J.

Dad and J's room, the study and ensuite were down one end of our house, while the other three bedrooms were down the other end, divided by a huge living/dining room, kitchen and another living room. Dad, J and K were always down 'their' end, while Sherry and I were relegated to the other end. K only slept in her room; she was with J down her end at all other times. I would quickly sit up straight and freeze as she passed through the hall on her way to put K to bed because I was worried I would get in trouble for something.

Sometimes we ate dinner all together at the dining table, but we preferred it when we were allowed to eat on our laps in front of the TV and they'd take their dinners down to their room; we could relax more that way. On very rare occasions, when there was an argument, dad might come and sit with us briefly on the couch. We loved it when he did. Most nights, though, Sherry and I would watch our TV while they were down their end, then brush our teeth and go down to knock on their door to say goodnight.

Their bedroom door at most times of the day and night was usually closed. That's certainly a metaphor. We had to knock and wait, even if K was already in there. We were discouraged from calling K our sister, or playing or engaging with her, other than to pose for a photo occasionally. Even then, it was a stiff pose, no arms cuddling each other or anything like that.

I remember one day, when K was a toddler, she came and sat between me and Sherry on the couch. J told us to 'give her room!' Some may say J was barely more than a child herself – but my sister and I really *were* children and we had no choice about the situation we were in.

Before we left Sydney for Coomera, I was given my first diary. I was just learning to write, but I would note down the things J would do or say to me. J read my diary and left a note next to an entry. 'She is the cat's mother,' she corrected me. Even my diary was a censored version of myself. Everything was controlled.

Our daily routine was a robotic succession, to ensure our obedience and minimal contact with J, K and our dad. We'd have to wait thirty minutes every afternoon after school for dad to finish teaching at his high school then pick us up on his way home. He used to buy us a thickshake *and* ice-cream sometimes from the petrol station across from the school. It was our secret from J and is perhaps when I started to equate sugar with love; this was a tough addiction to break. I remember really struggling to get through all of my dinner on these nights! But I knew it wasn't an option to leave food on the plate.

One positive outcome of not feeling wanted was that we had a lot of freedom once we'd left the property and were out of sight and mind. When we weren't at school or netball, we were told to go off for the day with a packed lunch; always one sandwich, one piece of fruit and one muesli bar. We'd go bike riding seven kilometres down to the river, to the shops or on various dirt tracks leading into the bush. In the backyard, we'd play on the tennis court and swim in the pool when we were allowed to stay around. We were lucky to have these and my father did spend some time with us in the pool, giving us backflips, and on the court, teaching us to play tennis. Neither J nor K went in the pool or on the court when we were there, though, that I remember.

I vividly remember how my sister and I would take each other around the pool on a floaty toy in a game we called Blue Lagoon Cruises. We took turns pretending to be the tour guide and the guest. I remember the feeling of being floated around, looking up at the sky and feeling weightless. That feeling would alter my state somehow. In those moments, I wasn't in my backyard, I was on a Blue Lagoon Cruise. I was somewhere else – relaxed and loving life.

A Dream

28th of August 2012
Byron Bay, New South Wales

I'm in the pool at Bayview with my dad and sister – and a shark. We're jumping out of the water when the shark bites my sister's leg. I see clearly and vividly its cold, emotionless eyes, its nose and teeth, and yell, 'Naughty shark!' I'm not afraid, but I hope it hasn't broken the skin.

CHAPTER THREE

This House Ain't A Home

Nanna Simms used to call us her sunshine girls. When Sherry and I visited her in Sydney, she'd open the door and rub her hands together in excitement, exclaiming, 'Oh, my sunshine girls!' She was so gorgeous; we really loved our Nanna and staying with her in the school holidays. We used to catch a bus from the Gold Coast to Casino and then the train down to Sydney on our own. Looking back, it was a pretty long way for two little girls to travel by themselves. But back then, it was all an adventure, and an escape from a tense home life. A couple of times our Mum's brother Greg and his wife Merilyn picked us up from the train station in Sydney and took us to Nanna's house in Clovelly. Nanna made a point of making us something from scratch each time we visited: lemon butter, butterfly cakes with thick cream, or biscuits with cornflakes and chocolate chips, Nanna's 'chock rocks'. It made us feel special that she'd made something just for us. Her pantry was always stocked with chocolates and sweets — and things we didn't have much access to at home in Coomera; it was heaven.

'Oh no, you'll make yourself sick eating all those sweets, and then your dad won't let you visit me anymore,' Nanna used to say. She was only half-joking. I think the fear of being cut off from us was very real for her.

I can't help but smile when I think of Nanna Simms. She had a big veggie garden out the back where she grew her own produce, which she'd pick and cook for dinner. She would let us dress up in her clothes and put on shows, and any time we saw a busker playing music on the street, she would give us coins to tip them. I still do that today.

While Nanna was a light in my childhood, I remember being scared of my grandfather. From my perspective, Pa seemed older than Nanna and he was quite strict. When he spoke, he talked for a long time but never really said much. We used to watch the cricket with him, bring him his 'elevenses' (morning tea) when Nanna asked us to, though I preferred to avoid him as much as possible. We didn't spend much quality time with him on our own. Sometimes a taxi would come and pick Pa up to take him to the club or a doctor's appointment, and I would feel this sense of relief when he left. It was just more comfortable when he wasn't there. Plus, we loved having our Nanna all to ourselves.

When Nanna made Pa his 'elevenses', usually crackers and cheese, she would see if she was granted permission to take us to the city to see a movie or something. If we were allowed, she would leave Pa with a hot lunch to heat up, and the fairly large quota of beer he was allowed each day. Nanna made sure we thanked him for letting us go and for paying for our movie. We had good manners so we would have anyway, but he made me anxious.

Nanna didn't sleep in the same bed as Pa; she had her own room. When Sherry and I visited, we would sleep in Nanna's room on a mattress each and she would set up a spare bed for herself in the enclosed veranda area.

I have one specific memory of an incident with Pa during one of our visits. I don't recall if this was a one-off incident, but it was certainly the last. I was sitting on my Pa's lap in his special chair in the tiny enclosed patio room near the entrance of the house, and I was reading a book to him. I was an advanced reader for my young age and Pa was encouraging me. 'Keep reading,' he instructed, while he touched me inappropriately.

Pa must've thought Nanna was down the other end of the house – and he was positioned so he could see her if she appeared in the hallway with enough time to stop. But Nanna had actually been in Pa's bedroom, more directly across from where we sat. She might've been making up the bed or something. She emerged from the bedroom and saw what was happening. It's the only time I ever saw my grandmother stand up to her husband in anger.

Nanna sent me to her room (where my sister and I would sleep) and I sat on the bed in shame, as though I'd done something wrong, and I feared being in trouble. I anxiously eavesdropped on their conversation. My sister was watching TV and I think came in to see what was happening; I don't recall what I told her.

When Nanna finally came to talk to me, she asked me not to tell anyone what had just happened and told me I wouldn't be reading to Pa ever again. Nanna was afraid my father wouldn't allow us to visit anymore, should he learn what had happened. These visits were her last living connection to her beloved daughter. I stayed silent and this memory got archived, along with the other unfathomable ones, until it would gradually seep back in.

A Dream

March 2012
At a Vipassana (Silent Meditation), Northern New South Wales

I'm with two known men. I am kissing a penis.

Back in Queensland, there was lots of yelling and arguments between J and my father, usually behind their closed door but not always. I remember my sister and I hunkering down in our rooms, or tensing up and waiting for the storm to pass.

There were often these icy silences where we barely dared to breathe or move to avoid getting in trouble. It was the same when we were in the car; the mood was dictated by whether there was music or silence. We learned to adapt to these variations – hypervigilance was birthed.

Around this time, J's dad came to visit us and meet his grandchild. It was a big deal, and my sister and I were warned to be on our best behaviour. J and my father wanted to make a good impression on her dad, and they really wanted him to like my father. I assume J's dad didn't approve of their marriage as he didn't come to their wedding. I think he actually disowned J for a period of time because we hadn't met him or heard from him up until this point.

During the visit, J's dad took us all out to dinner at Sanctuary Cove, which he paid for. I think the meeting must have gone well, because not long after, J's dad sent us a painting for our house. Although, I don't remember seeing him ever again.

In February 1990, K had just turned five when J prepared her van for a journey to Sydney. She told us she was taking K to visit her mum, but she didn't return.

Dad showed big emotions – the only time I remember him doing so. He sent J a soppy Michael Bolton song and a love letter begging her to return. He got really depressed and told us if he didn't have us girls, he would've killed himself. I was twelve and it was eight years after my Mother disappeared. He said he wished he'd tried harder with our Mother to make it work, as he said this, he was crying.

Dad's sadness over losing J soon turned to anger, once he realised she wasn't going to return. Since it was J's mum who initially took her in, my father felt betrayed and villainised by her as well, making us get rid of all the gifts J's mum had ever given us, sending them all back to her.

Next ensued a nasty custody battle (between J and my dad) over K. I recall dad calling J a 'bitch', and the female psychologist from the shelter she was staying in who was helping her, a 'charlatan'. He'd play the distraught victim as he read the newspaper articles, which stereotyped him as brutish because of the boots he was wearing in court and his outdated suit. His only 'good' pair of shoes was an old pair of boots (my dad was a sneakers or thongs guy).

I'd sometimes overhear snippets of conversations with Paul or his parents. My father told us that there were some allegations against him and asked us if we believed them. We were young and gullible; we loved our dad and perceived he was the good guy in all of this. Years later, I would learn that J called my father controlling and abusive and that she was 'scared he would get rid of her, like he got rid of his first wife'. He claims the allegations were to cast doubt in the court's mind, in order for J to gain custody over K. I believed him.

I had no idea that after J left my father, she had gone to the police to make a statement about my Mother. I've since found out that J met up with my Mother's brother Greg and his wife Merilyn after she moved back to Sydney. She'd reached out to Nanna Simms, who had understandably declined to speak with her, but Greg and Merilyn felt it was probably important that they listen to what J had to say to them about my father. This is the story she told them, which she relayed to the police on the 17th of May 1990 …

Sometime in late 1981, J says she went on a trip with my father, who had picked her up from school in his car. She was wearing her school uniform. J remembers them driving over the Harbour Bridge, to an unfamiliar suburb 'out West'. When the car came to a stop, J says she could see a chain wire fence and a building with a few steps up to it. She did not see any signage. J says dad told her to wait in the car while he went into the building. He wasn't gone for very long, perhaps fifteen or twenty minutes. When he returned to the car he said, 'I went inside to get a hitman to kill Lyn, but then I decided I couldn't do it because innocent people would be hurt.'

While I don't doubt that this could've happened, I always thought that last sentence was a strange thing to say (obviously someone would be very hurt!) nor his real reason for not following through (or did he?); more likely it was because he didn't want to part with the money!

After the story was told to the police, my Mother's case was reopened. But there wasn't much to 'reopen'. When they dug up the case file, it was almost empty.

In January 1991, my father was interviewed by police at Beenleigh Station in Queensland. In the interviews, he dropped the names of police officers he knew on the Northern Beaches.

Back in Bayview, police did a survey of our old home using ground-penetrating radar focusing on the area around the swimming pool. No digging was done, and nothing was found. I wonder what the new owners of our old house thought of it all. Apparently, they had started doing some work to the property the year before – including pouring concrete – and my father had visited the house and quizzed the owners about where they would be digging.

The woman who bought Paul's house – which was just down the street and backed onto bushland like ours – took a bone her dogs had dug up to the police station to be tested. She'd heard the story of my Mother and feared the worst. The tests revealed the bone was animal.

It was dead end after dead end.

In Coomera, life went on without J. And without our beautiful Mother.

My dad didn't cook. He always had someone to do it for him, until we found ourselves alone for the first time. Not long after J left my father, when I was about thirteen, my well-meaning home economics teacher in high school kindly donated to me some recipe books while saying to me, 'Now that you're the woman of the house, you need to learn to cook for your dad.' She was coming from a different mindset, but in my opinion, she should have handed my father the fucking cookbooks and told him to learn how to cook! I didn't take over the cooking; instead we ate a lot of frozen dinners and takeaways until he got a new girlfriend. It was *not* my job as a thirteen-year-old girl to take care of my father!

I don't know how long my dad was single, but it was a much happier time for me and my sister while he was. There was a sense of being able to breathe more easily once J was gone and the tension in the house had lifted. My father taught me how to jive, so whenever I hear the song 'Runaround Sue', it always reminds me of him. It was a happy memory. We got more attention from our dad, which I'm sure we were craving, and loved it when K came for half the holidays and we were allowed to call her our sister and engage with her, even cuddle her!

J left behind her cassette tapes and I remember hoarding them in my room; I was like a pirate with newfound treasure. I sat on the carpet in my bedroom, with the small boom box (probably also J's), huddled down in the narrow gap between my single bed and the full-sized window, enjoying the new freedom of choosing and playing music. I loved my dad's music – the Bee Gees, the Hollies, Creedence Clearwater Revival, etc – but when I listened to this new genre of music – Pink Floyd, Deep Purple and Carole King – it expanded me somehow and left me feeling something I don't quite have words for. I still remember that feeling.

It was an escape from a reality I didn't even know was toxic, it was hope, it was expansion into a whole new universe and way of seeing things. So, I guess I have J to thank for that. In J's absence, my sister and I could walk around the house freely. We could be. I remember playing my father's records on the giant stereo in the living room, finally being allowed to live in and move around the whole house! The freedom extended to my father's study, which included a book on Edgar Cayce and reincarnation. It held truth and activated what I would describe as remembrance in me. That was possibly the beginning of my 'spiritual seeking'.

We weren't a religious family, but my dad was open to some of these concepts, such as spirits and reincarnation. It was around this age I would write deep ponderings in my diaries such as, 'Why are we here (in this world)? Where did we come from and where do we go when we die?'

I became best friends with a girl in primary school whose family were born again Christians. I had fairly regular sleepovers at her house, and I went to church with them a handful of times. On one of those occasions, my friend and I got kicked out of children's church for hiding (we thought we were being funny, apparently we were not), so as we went to where the adults were, I witnessed a room full of people speaking in tongues, and apparently became born again. I began to fear demons and the devil, though I suspect that J allowing us to watch *The Omen* when we were waaayyy too young may have contributed. It haunted me for years and to this day I don't think I've watched another horror movie or psychological thriller (ironically, perhaps, because my earlier life was one)! I began praying to Jesus to protect me. One weekend I came home and started crying, telling my dad I was sad because he was going to go to hell when he died because he wasn't born again. He was quite tolerant and explained to me that he didn't believe that. The conversation marked the end of the church visits, and different high schools put an end to that friendship naturally anyway.

My sister and I were finally living in a peaceful house with our dad all to ourselves, but it didn't last long. When dad met a woman on an organised singles date night, things moved too quickly for me. This woman and her teenage son moved into our home at Coomera almost instantly, and she and my father started planning their wedding within a very short period of time. She was the person who took me shopping to buy my first bra, in place of my Mum.

Sadly for her, she copped my just-turned-teen attitude as I resisted the rapid changes being forced upon us. Looking back, she was actually quite nice, albeit very open at times, which was in stark contrast to the closed-door policy we'd grown up with during dad's marriage to J. My dad's new fiancée was quite comfortable with nudity and would sometimes answer the door not completely dressed. One day (or night) I heard her and my father having sex behind their closed bedroom door. I had heard her yelling; thinking she was hurt, I very naively went running down the hall to see if she was okay! Thankfully I realised before I knocked! This confused my young mind and the next night at dinner I called her a slut. She told me to leave, so as I left the table with my dinner plate in hand, she came to slap me across the face. I instinctually raised my arms in self-defence and my plate accidentally clipped her chin. She was okay – dad took her to the hospital and she required a few stitches – but that was the end of that partnership. Her older son came to collect her minimal belongings and we never saw her again.

Dad later thanked me, though I certainly hadn't intended on ending the relationship. He admitted he was in a bit of a desperate state when he met her and could see in hindsight that they weren't really a good match.

CHAPTER FOUR

The Cracks Appear

I got my first part-time job at thirteen. The Coomera pharmacy hadn't been looking for an employee but were impressed by my initiative when I enquired and hired me to clean the shelves, then started to train me on the register. I was paid $3 an hour and worked seven hours a week. Twenty-one dollars a week felt like a lot of money at the time! My dad would take me there after school twice a week and on Saturday mornings. He was proud of me with my good work ethic.

I got bored of the job after a while and moved on to another, while also babysitting for our neighbours. Becoming bored easily would go on to become a pattern in my life and is likely why I always have an assortment of various, eclectic jobs – unlike the other people in my family who were all solid in their professional careers, many of them as teachers.

Enter stage right: S, a maths and science teacher from my high school. My father asked her on a date to a fancy dress party and she accepted. They went as Richard Gere and Julia Roberts in *Pretty Woman*. Great, this meant I had a father, uncle, auntie, cousins and soon to be stepmother all at the same high school. S had two children, boy and girl twins around the same age as K, who was five. She was highly intelligent but was also never wrong, just like my father. She and my father were both control freak perfectionists. She had beautiful antique furniture … you know, the kind with the couch that kids aren't allowed to sit on – oh so homely! She was really good at crafts, was an amazing cook and also enjoyed designing the lovely red brick, colonial style house she and my father would build together on the Gold Coast.

They met while we were still living in Coomera, but I don't remember if S and her kids ever came to live with us there or not. Dad had to sell Coomera to pay J out for their divorce settlement; obviously he was bitter about that, but I think a fresh start in a new place was a necessary good thing. We lived in S's parents' house for six months while they travelled, and we built a new family home.

A Memory

I'm driving home to Coomera with my father and sister. I'm about fourteen, and we're likely coming home from Friday night family dinner at Nandi and Pop's house, or possibly netball training. At the sharp bend in the road, where it would sometimes flood (and when it did, on rare occasions, we would get to miss school), dad says something I'll never forget. I don't remember the context of the conversation, I just remember vividly the line my father spoke and the creepy feeling it gave me at the time. Each time I think about it, it ignites that fire in my belly which on auto pilot, I smother out. He said: 'It's a shame your mother let herself go; she had such a pretty face.'

I was in my early teens when Dad and S got married in Fiji in 1993. A couple of days before the wedding, the family were gathered in our wooden, thatched-roof hut while a cyclone raged outside. My soon-to-be stepbrother slept through the commotion of water coming in on the floor while we were all lifting our suitcases onto the beds to keep them dry. The palm trees were swept sideways as we formed a human chain to follow an invisible path. My dad led us all out of the flooded hut as we couldn't see far in front of us, and got us safely to the main part of the hotel. I can't recall feeling scared at all; it seems I'm good with these types of storms, just not the emotional kind.

The day of the wedding arrived and lucky for them, other than the sea being brown, the grounds had all been cleared and the tropics were beautiful again.

Paul and his family came to Fiji for the wedding, as did S's parents. Paul and S used to butt heads a lot and I would say this eventually put more distance between him and my dad (with my dad and S eventually moving away from Paul and his family for the first time in my father's and Paul's lives).

That distance might not have been all S's doing. I have wondered if, on some deep psychological level, looking at the 'mirror' of themselves was a constant reminder for my father of what he'd done.

In our new home on the Gold Coast, I seemed to cop harsh criticism from S, which I didn't take lying down, having reached saturation point of non-nurturing women in my life. Compared to my sister, who got along okay with S, I was more difficult to control, and I'm sure I was quite challenging in my own ways. S's own daughter was perfect, of course, but her son certainly copped it from my father as well. I believe my father was jealous of the attention S gave to him and perceived he was a 'Mumma's boy', so took it upon himself to 'toughen him up'. Or possibly − again on some deep psychological level − maybe dad was trying to prevent S's son from turning out like he did?

That was the first time I started observing glimpses of deeply concerning traits in my father; up until then he had been my hero and could do no wrong. He would bully my stepbrother and pretend to 'play' rough with him, scowling at him not to be a sissy if he started to cry. I'd catch a glimpse of the dark look in his eyes and knew he wasn't playing. It gave me an uncomfortable feeling in my solar plexus that I kept having to override but would someday be unable to ignore.

I would regularly stand up for my stepbrother because I could see what was really happening and felt I understood him.

During this time, I felt the absence of my Mother often. When I got my first period, I didn't tell anyone. I kept the knowledge to myself as a sacred little powerplay. When my stepmother said something condescending to me like, 'How would you know, you're only a child!' I revealed with scorn that I was no longer a child. My father got a bit emotional and sentimental, and I was angry at them both, not even knowing that what I needed right then was my Mum.

My father would only ever mention my Mum when S mentioned her ex-husband. Although I was in my early teens by then and unaware of the concept of emotional intelligence, I thought my father was like an ego-centred little child, hoping that the mention of her might trigger a mirrored jealous response. It angered me that he used my Mother's memory as bait in that way, never to honour or pay respect to her, or to bring comfort and share her with her two daughters.

I was, however, programmed to be 'nice' and 'happy' as all good little girls are and shoved these observations down into a deep, dark inner hole to be preserved for future exploration, along with my other treasure trove of inner knowings and rememberings. Survival is a powerful force, albeit a charade at times.

I grew up believing the story we were told – that our Mother left us of her own free will. Though by this point I believed she must've had mental illness or amnesia to have stayed away for so long. As well as telling us Mum left because she didn't love us anymore, dad also spun a story about Mum running off with the Hare Krishnas. When I was nineteen, I visited a Hare Krishna temple in Murwillumbah and found myself looking around at the women's faces, somewhat hoping to see my Mother's eyes mirrored back at me. I danced outside as the Hare Krishnas chanted and gazed up at the stars. 'Where are you, Mum?' I implored to the universe. 'Where *are* you?' I felt the deep longing for my Mother amplified in that moment, as I called out for her from the black hole, as vast as the night sky.

The disgusting lies I was told as a child must have tasted like bitter poison, but one day I would feel compelled enough to reclaim those difficult truths.

On the surface I appeared fine; I did well academically, athletically, in my chosen extra-curricular activities, part-time job and socially in my teens. But around this time I did write in my diary and on my hand: 'life sux and I want to die'. I believe it was while my father and S were still dating that we went on a family holiday to Coffs Harbour, New South Wales. We'd gone to a nearby beach at Sawtell where I'd crossed the channel on my surfboard and was learning to surf on the whitewash. As I embarked to return to my family, a strong rip swept me away and giant waves washed me over the rocks, where my father stood to try to help me. What happened for me was at that moment, just before I was swept along the rocks, time stood still. I felt as though I was being offered the chance to leave the Earth, to die. I felt a loving, feminine presence – perhaps an angel, a spirit guide or my Mother? She felt kind but also firm and centred. My response to her and to what I felt was the choice at hand, was as clear as day: 'No, I don't want to leave yet, *I haven't done what I came here to do.*' I don't recall her exact words to me, but they were something along the lines of, 'Well then, get on with it ...' The response was a little less direct than that, but the meaning remains the same. So no longer did I say I wanted to die, though I still felt and wrote that 'life sux'. Immediately afterward, I sulked in self-pity in the back of the minivan, scraped and slightly bloody from head to toe and without a loving Mother to hug and hold me and make the world safe again.

Unfortunately, I didn't have the maturity or the communication skills to have a better relationship with S, and after a few years of conflict between us, all I could manage in my defence was to tell her to fuck off and I started to rebel against what I felt were tight reins, strangleholding my freedom. I admit I was probably difficult to parent in many ways, unable to allow myself to be put down anymore.

My father would sometimes stand up for me and this would cause arguments between him and S as well, though they argued a lot about other things too. This was a tumultuous time and my father told me that I was going to be the cause of his third marriage breakup if I didn't change, so at seventeen I left home.

I had just finished high school, had a wild, fun schoolies, bought my first car, and was waitressing at Sanctuary Cove while waiting to start university. My father helped me move the contents of my room into a share house where two of my cousins and four other people lived. Prior to leaving home I'd got my driver's licence and entered the realms of sweet, joyous partial independence, but leaving home was one of the best feelings in the world. It certainly had its challenges – both emotionally and in supporting myself financially while studying, working two to four part-time jobs – but we still had *wayyy* too much fun!! It was an epic time of self-discovery and absolute freedom beyond my most beautiful imaginings.

When I moved out of home, I didn't get invited back for dinners by my father or his wife, other than for birthdays and such. S and I seemed glad to be free of each other and the constant conflict, though her criticism of me continued into adulthood, until the last time I saw her. I'd never known such joyous freedom, though I paradoxically sank into cyclical depressions, which I have since come to understand.

A Memory

I'm driving with my father, this time in my late teens. I innocently make a comment to him: 'I just get the intuition that you need to forgive yourself for something.' An intensely questioning look comes over his face. He turns to stare directly at me, and his eyes look deep inside me. He's searching for something. I don't know it in the moment, but I now believe he was looking at me to see if I knew. Did I know what he'd done? Did I know what happened to my Mum?

When dad gets the reassurance he needs from my blank face, he visibly relaxes. He responds with an offhand comment, 'Yeah, probably.'

I went to my first meditation group when I was nineteen. I was living with a friend on the Gold Coast. At the group, I felt the presence of someone standing at my shoulder but when I opened my eyes, there was no-one there. I guess some emotions came up to be felt and as I walked home, I tripped on some uneven part of the driveway and hurt myself. It was exactly what I needed, as it triggered deep tears that needed to be released and had been held onto for so long. Though at this time, I had no idea what was about to unfold in my life or why I was crying such massive tears.

I was studying at university at the time. I had wanted to do social work but hadn't got a good enough entry score for the degree, so I applied to do primary school teaching with the intention of swapping over once in the course. I resisted being a teacher because the majority of my family were teachers and I thought it seemed too unoriginal. I always loved children, though, and worked with them consistently from a young age as a babysitter, and later in a job at 'After School and Vacation Care', then working alongside another lady in a Behaviour Management role in schools. When I did my first teaching prac, I absolutely loved it and stuck with the degree for the next (almost) four years.

I saw a lot of flaws in the education system at the time and although it has improved, I still believe it needs a massive overhaul (as do many outmoded systems in our patriarchal society) as it tries to make children all fit a particular mould or otherwise fail, rewarding only a particular type of success and programming them to be obedient straight-line thinkers for our economy-driven society. I believed I could try to play my part to create positive change in this regard, from inside the system. A little idealistic of me, perhaps?

During the second year of my degree, when I was nineteen, I met someone who I will call 'Ian', my first long-term boyfriend. My uni friend and I had been flitting down the street in Surfers Paradise on the Gold Coast on a night out and Ian had been drawn to my free-spirited abandon, and assumed I must've been from Northern New South Wales as I definitely wasn't a stereotypical Gold Coast 'type'. We chatted fairly extensively and exchanged numbers, then later went on to be in a relationship for the next three and a half years. In the very beginning of the relationship, Ian cheated on me with his ex-girlfriend. This probably should've been the end, but I thought I had the maturity to forgive and give him another chance as he seemed genuinely regretful. The betrayal and anger I felt toward him stayed with me though and tainted our connection, as did several other factors. What I have come to understand as true for myself is that the frequency of trust has a purity, a super clear, high vibration. Once that trust has been broken, I don't feel it ever returns to that absolute pure state again. Perhaps some people are able to move past such things, but for me, complete honesty and trust is paramount and crucial in building a solid foundation for a healthy relationship. Obviously, what I have seen occur in my Mother and father's relationship – the violence and infidelity – will also have affected my psyche at its very core.

Though I have dearly loved all of my boyfriends and would still give each and every one a hug if we met up again (most I've remained friends with, though we live on different continents), I can see the patterns of attracting men with unresolved trauma, mirroring my own. I see the cycles of emotional abuse, from both sides, though I was oblivious to that fact at the time. None of my relationships have been physically abusive, but unhealthy relationships are what was modelled for me. When I was younger, I knew I wanted different, but I didn't know yet how to get there. So I rode the emotional roller-coaster and learned lessons the hard way.

At uni, by the time I reached my last and final prac, I wasn't doing that great. I struggled with discipline, boundaries and assessing the kids – all of the left-brain aspects of the job. In my defence, my mentor teacher had me for a previous prac and thought I had it down, so had been leaving me alone with the kids when she shouldn't have and perhaps could have been a little more present to pick up on the fact I was flailing. At twenty-one or so years of age, I wasn't humble enough to admit it either. I had also broken up with Ian, but we had agreed to stay living together for practical purposes until the end of my degree. My car decided that would be a good time to break down, so my now ex-boyfriend was kindly driving me to and from my last six-week prac *and* my dear Pop Dawson died!

Just weeks before he died of a heart attack, I had accompanied my Pop to the funeral of one of his friends, where we'd held hands and he tried to make me promise I wouldn't cry when he died. I didn't promise, as I knew myself better than that. It was only a short time later that he passed. I did cry, but the family all agreed to wear colourful clothes instead of black to his funeral and tell 'Pop' jokes in his honour. His passing affected me deeply, as he was a loving support in my life and always checked in to see how I was. He lent me his car when my car was written off by a bus (I wasn't at fault), so I could still get to uni and work. Pop always had a listening ear for his family; he loved us all very much.

It was too much for me all at once. I was two weeks away from finishing my final prac, and hence my four-year degree, but I would've got a poor rating, which would have made it harder to gain good employment. If I'd known then what I know now – that I simply wasn't cut out for that type of career – I would've completed the degree with the poor rating and still held that piece of paper in my hands.

It was at a weekly spiritual group where someone told me they sensed Colorado around me. I resisted, as I had no intention of travelling to the USA at that point. Shortly after the spiritual group meeting, I was reading a book about Atlantis that mentioned Colorado. 'Interesting,' I noted. Then, I saw a notice in my local newspaper advertising a nannying position for a family in Colorado in the foothills of the Rocky Mountains. I applied for the position and when I got it, I decided I would take a year off from my degree and come back for a fresh start after my time abroad.

I had been to Malaysia, Fiji and Thailand on family trips, but this was the first time I'd gone overseas on my own. It wasn't that hard to say goodbye to my family because at some point during those years, my family had relocated to Yeppoon, Queensland. Because I was working lots during the uni holidays, I didn't seem them often anyway. So, in May 2000, I dissolved a majority of my Australian ties and flew to Denver, Colorado, where I would be living in an alpine forested town called Evergreen.

Before I left, I registered my Mother with the Salvation Army, who have a Family Tracing Service that actively works to reunite missing people with their families. I gave them two of the precious few photos I had of my Mum. Unfortunately, the photos weren't returned to me before I moved overseas. I had lost them, just like I lost my Mum.

CHAPTER FIVE

Outside the Sphere of Influence

I remember my first morning in Evergreen, waking up jetlagged, the insulated quiet of the springtime snow surrounding my new home. It smelt of pine and juniper and I gaped in awe at the sight of chipmunks flitting on the deck and herds of elk crossing the meadow to nibble on some nearby greenery.

I was initially hired by a family with two daughters, aged two and four – the same age my sister and I were when our Mother 'left us'. This certainly was a wakeup call and made me so sad, to think of us so young and still needing our Mother's nurturing and love; I could tangibly understand the impact it would've had, for that love to be taken away so abruptly and prematurely at such vulnerable and dependent ages. Though at this stage, I still believed my Mum was very much alive and out in the world somewhere.

For various reasons, things hadn't worked out at my first nannying job, and I ended up with a different wonderful family with two boys (and a little girl to be born in the coming years). Still to this day, I love the family dearly and am in occasional contact with them. The mum was lovely, very personable and eager to meet me. My memory of meeting the dad is one of my favourite recollections of him. He was sitting all relaxed by a pool, stretching out his limbs from the confines of his deck chair, hands behind head, when he said to me, 'Yeah, we do alright, we make good money, but we don't think it makes us better than anybody else.' Maybe this might work out okay, then …?

The mum was a lobbyist and required a nanny while she was in session for six months out of the year. So, I would be with them for those six months, then travel and live in my van, doing odd jobs and living in communities for the other six months. I did a variety of things during this time, including waitressing, retail work, markets, massage, painting, gardening and working at Renaissance Festivals, which was lots of fun. I loved working with the kids and became a quirky part of their family.

I had my first white Christmas in Colorado, which even included a horse-drawn sleigh ride with the kids, before flitting off for a warmer New Year's Eve escape in Florida. A man I met there at a hostel told me about an intentional community in the Canary Islands and gave me detailed instructions on how to get there. I wrote the directions down verbatim in the back of my journal: fly to Tenerife, catch a boat to San Sebastian (de La Gomera), jump on a bus to the town of La Playa Caies, Shwiner Bokt (Bay of Pigs) and hitchhike through the Valle Gran Rey (Valley of the King) up north, to arrive at Finca Argayall, which means 'Place of Light'. Every time I got a new journal, I copied the instructions into it and carried them with me, alongside stories of my adventures. The 'Place of Light' sounded like my kind of place.

Back in Colorado, I fostered a dog named 'Taz' and when I asked him if he was 'the one', he sat on my lap and his previous foster carer let me take him on the spot. Definitely one of the big loves of my life!

There were numerous hiking trails in that area that we frequented regularly, as well as lots of amazing live music and regular drum circles. I was loving life! I had great friends and lovely boyfriends (in singular procession, haha), though my experiences of the past had given me a fear of commitment – something I would come to understand in future years and after much inward self-recovery.

During my 'time off' from nannying, I loved hopping in my van, with everything I owned and needed in my immediate vicinity, and choosing where I'd go on a whim. One place I chose because of its name and the fact there were hot springs there, was the town of Truth or Consequences in New Mexico, the 'Land of Enchantment' where it smells like brush sage and dry, mineral-rich red/orange dirt.

I'd need a whole other book to tell of these adventures, but a few highlights are: driving in my green kombi, listening to the song by Led Zeppelin, 'Over the Hills and Far Away', where there's a line about gazing along the open road. I'm rocking out, feeling blissfully happy as I look out the window at one of the most spectacular sunsets I've ever seen reflecting off the white salt marshes of the Great Salt Lake in Utah.

SO many sunsets, so many sing-alongs and crazy, fun adventures!

I was driving the green kombi in Colorado on a major freeway one day, when I heard the name 'Kiala' whispered. I wasn't on any drugs or anything and am not usually psychically auditory. I have no idea what, why or who …? But I loved the name so much, I named my kombi that, painted it on her boot and decided if I ever had a daughter, I would like to name her Kiala, provided it suited her.

In 2001, I was in Colorado where I was housesitting for a family, on a lovely spring day when I felt a strong urge to write my Nanna Simms a letter. I sat under a tree among some green grass in the wild-flowered meadow and found myself pouring out my love for her onto those pages. All of our happy memories flowed out from me, including everything I loved about her – especially her big, beautiful, nurturing tummy that she'd frowned upon, whereas for me, it had held me safe and softly squished in her love. Months later when I was living in my campervan, I was at a Renaissance Festival in Minnesota when I dreamed my Nanna Simms had come to me in my dreams and told me what had happened to my dear Mum. When I woke, I immediately lost any knowing of what she'd said, but the feeling stayed with me that she now knew. When I checked my emails later that day, there was a message from Auntie Pat, informing me that Nanna had passed.

I am told that she carried my letter in her purse until she passed over, not long after I wrote it. I wish I had kept a copy.

My Nanna never stopped looking for her daughter. One of the places my father said my Mother had run away to was the Central Coast, so Nanna would go there to look for her. She took flyers and would stop people in the street to ask if they'd seen my Mother. She used to catch the train because she didn't drive. It was a lengthy trip, but that didn't stop her. She was determined to find answers, to find her daughter, to find peace.

Nanna died without ever knowing what happened to her daughter.

The same year Nanna died, a coronial inquest was launched into my Mother's case after investigations by the police remained inconclusive.

Detective Damian Loone had been handed the case in 1998, but because the case records had been 'poorly' compiled and stored, the investigation basically had to start over.

One of the first things they did was tap my father's phone while the interviews and searches were going on, in the hope that he'd reveal something in conversations. But he didn't say a single word about the reopening of the police investigation or Mum's disappearance. He didn't say, 'Wow, how about all this police stuff in the papers?' or 'Here's hoping the police can find Lyn.' Not a word. His silence spoke volumes.

To Detective Paul Hume, who was Damian's boss at the time, the silence said: 'Guilty as sin.'

In 2000, the police conducted an excavation dig in a small area around the pool at our old home in Bayview. They found a woman's pink cardigan in pieces. The cardigan appeared to have slash marks. The crime scene investigation officer, Bob Gibbs, has said the slashes were consistent 'with knife marks in a domestic stabbing'.

Our neighbour Julie Andrew knew the cardigan well; it was my Mum's favourite, she said. No DNA was found on the cardigan, though, so it became another dead end. It's baffling to me that after they found the cardigan, they didn't dig around the whole pool. Apparently, local police had wanted to keep digging, but because of costs and potentially other reasons, they were not allowed.

After three years of investigating the case, Damian took it to the coroner, with the hope that he'd found enough evidence for a ruling to be made. At the coronial inquest, Deputy State Coroner Jan Stevenson concluded that my Mother had been murdered by a known person, and that person was my father. The coroner recommended charges be laid, but the Director of Public Prosecutions (DPP) at the time didn't feel there was enough for any charges to stick.

I was largely oblivious to all that was occurring and was being reported fairly widely in the media over in Australia. News of the inquest didn't make it over to America – no news from Australia did – Mum's family mentioned it in their emails, but I didn't understand the magnitude of it. My distance to the case may have been due to circumstances or my subconscious choosing, because I wasn't ready to face the truth yet.

A Poem

November 2002
Colorado, USA

X Marks the Spot

If I left before my time, would I want more?
Leaving before the game, no chance to score
Losing myself, I find
Self constraints I bind
Depths of infinity, shall I go?
The more I think, the less I know
Dwelling on borrowed highways of slime
Here nor there, guilty of undefinable crime
Shan't be led astray by thought nor thread
Receiving rewards for which I'm bred
Hollow construction paves roads of destruction
Leaving the path to create my own, necessary function
Being and doing too many moments like this
Hoping for my prince, many frogs I have kissed
With the cleansing to erase old lines
Turning always to love for cues and signs
Castles, I have made drifting in the airs
This moment, I name time to build the stairs.

The happy moments in my life are usually chased by a darkness. Depression is cyclical for me, and it would dip in and out regularly. In those days I could hold it off until a weekend or lock myself away from the world, solitude being the most immediate relief in some ways, though I didn't recognise that what I was experiencing was actually depression, as initially it wasn't as debilitating and all-encompassing as it came to be.

In the September of 2004, my Uncle Paul and Auntie Marilyn were visiting New York, so I flew from Colorado to see them. I'm not a city person, so was amazed at how much I loved my three days in the vibrant, insanely busy city. I bought a small *djembe* (African drum) for my boyfriend at the time and walked the streets with it. I was stopped a few times for someone to bust out a rhythm – music is connection. I saw a musical with my auntie and uncle and caught a boat to see the Statue of Liberty en route. I then stayed with a friend on her boat on Long Island for a few days, Mama Ocean rocking me to sleep in her arms while singing me silent, salty lullabies.

Before I'd gone to New York, a friend had rescued a pregnant cat and it seemed that one of the kittens chose me, as I was the only person she purred for. Upon my return, when she still wasn't adopted by anybody else, she came on board with my gypsy ways and was the coolest travelling cat ever. Jezebel was her name. Yet another misconstrued and incorrectly portrayed strong female character, in my opinion!

She used to hike with my dog and myself and would claim the front seat, demoting my dog reluctantly to the floor. I also had a beautiful snake companion for a stint, who I named Ivy. She used to love the warmth of my neck and would hide in my hair, but she didn't enjoy the travelling part so much. Apparently, snakes need their stillness, something I also highly value now, so I found her a home in a classroom. My time with her – and taking the kids to the zoo – solidified my objection to keeping non-domestic animals in captivity for our own entertainment, unless for rehabilitation.

While there were moments when I missed my Australian family, there was something so freeing about not having familiar ties, no expectations around celebrations, or checking in every week. There was a real freedom for me in living my life exactly as I chose, with nobody criticising me or feeling disappointed in my choices, no obligation or faking it. In my time off from my nannying and waitressing jobs, I didn't have to be anywhere or answer to anyone. It was just me and the open road (and my dog and cat).

This is not to say life didn't have its challenges, it always does … I always drove older vehicles and they would regularly break down, but I managed to get through those moments okay and I give so much gratitude to the kind people who stopped to help me along the way.

My sister took a big year off while I was in the States to travel around to various places and she intentionally came to America to visit with me as well. I was living in Eugene,

Oregon, at the time, in the Pacific Northwest's temperate rainforest, with its luscious hot springs, large conifer trees, creeks, rivers and waterfalls and so many various types of moss and lichen. I was living in what we called an 'unintentional community' in one of six or so wooden yurts. There was a bathroom and kitchen in the main house, which was down a short trail through the aspen/birch-looking trees.

I was in a big love, albeit a slightly unhealthy relationship at the time and my sister arrived during the honeymoon phase. I love my sister dearly, but unfortunately for her, she represented a direct link to our family, most specifically our father, which triggered a stress response in my being. I didn't understand that at the time, but my sister picked up on it and felt unwelcome and hurt by the initial underlying lack of enthusiasm I had displayed. I took a break from the childminding and gardening I was doing at the time, and we had some good times together. We visited a coastal cave which was full of seals; the noise of their acoustically enhanced barking combined with the overwhelming fish stench was extremely primal. We also slid down a snow hill in garbage bags and giggled our heads off.

I really wanted to feel that closeness with her, and certainly that was there in an underlying, unspoken way for me. But we are on such contrasting wavelengths and completely different in how we express our emotions. I don't remember saying goodbye to my sister when she left to return to Australia, but we would've shared a big hug, and in my heart, that familiar tug of bittersweet … a fertile combination of sadness and relief at her leaving.

When I left Eugene with my 'big love' to visit Hawaii for the first time, it was on a two-week vacation, at the very end of December 2006. Hawaii was the closest I've felt to home. I love her tropical, luscious abundance, the fiery, volcanic, warrioress-inducing lands and waterfalls that merge with ocean waters to create pools made from fantasies. When my boyfriend and I landed on Maui it was night. We walked directly across to the beach with our backpacks and slept for the night under the stars, praying it wouldn't rain as it so often does in the tropics. I woke up into a dream and thought I was still sleeping. The vast, emerald green mountains, cascading down into the turquoise, north Pacific Ocean, coconut palms and wafts of sweetgrass fill the air; her lands are much softer in essence than Australia for me. My boyfriend and I were stuck in the same emotionally abusive patterns that were familiar to me – the honeymoon phase which cycles into a nightmare. It was unresolved trauma, but at that stage of my life, I didn't know how to break the cycle, nor did I have the awareness that's what I was in.

After yet another argument with my boyfriend, I wrote a poem by the light of the half-moon. Ironically, the poem is dated the 8th of January 2006, the anniversary of losing my Mother.

A Poem

8th of January 2006
Little Beach, Maui, Hawaii, USA

Does it make you angry because you feel it's true
The power of truth concealed
Your anger seeping into me Burns
Scalds, awakens old wounds
I've worked hard to hide from myself
Buried deep, I dig, it's repulsive
But the message of the toad as told,
Is to see the beauty in the seemingly ugly.
I tap into my high priestess worlds
I spill words to still fears
I open wounds to have Ocean waves lick them clean
I bathe in Moonlight's arms
As she holds me tight and lights my way
I'm learning to explore darkness with curiosity
The bitterness on my tongue
Fear present and lodged in my throat
But with the deep inner knowing of myself
Of who I am and what I choose
My whole self, I allow to touch me
Enter the womb of the unknown, the cave where darkness dwells
And I embrace it in order to bring back the light.

After a memorable trip to Mexico and Guatemala, I was returning to Colorado in order to be present for dear friends who were preparing to give birth. My new French-Canadian boyfriend and I were driving my Toyota camper from Arizona and although I'd had the vehicle checked by a mechanic before we left, it ceased to make 'the strange noise' once in the shop. So, we were driving along the freeway when a wheel bearing locked up and the entire rear axle came off the back. I looked in the rear-view mirror and realised it wasn't just a flat tyre; sparks were flying. A giant semi-trailer had swerved to avoid the tyre rolling across the road and pulled over with us to put the fire out. I was praying to the Angels and felt completely calm the whole time, as were my dog and cat. It was a miracle that the bunged-up corner remained intact and that we managed to find a mechanic whose friend lived nearby and just happened to have a rear axle that would fit my camper. The same camper also had a top corner of cedar shingles from where I'd slightly reversed into the edge of a barn while living in Oregon; my lovely carpenter roommate at the time helped with that one.

Back in Colorado, in the same camper – luckily on winding mountain roads and only doing 30mph – I was required to brake for a deer, not an uncommon occurrence ... but the mountain lion who'd been chasing the deer then clipped the edge of the camper and rebounded off and out of sight. My boyfriend and I looked at each other in disbelief. What shall we do?! He grabbed the only weapon available –

a broomstick – and ventured outside to see if we needed to call a wildlife carer for help. The mountain lion was nowhere to be seen, but had left a small tuft of fur as a souvenir in the metal trim on the corner of the camper.

I had many realisations while living in America, both big and small. I remember visiting my friend's family with her in Minnesota and witnessing what it's like to be loved and accepted unconditionally, the absolute freedom in being able to be completely herself and still feel embraced, appreciated and valued ... It was a real eye-opener for me to see them all at ease and laughing and loving each other – her feeling a sense of belonging and of always having a home to return to, with open arms awaiting her. I didn't feel that in my family.

I visited many psychics over the years, always asking where my Mother was. I received multiple different responses. One reader I saw in Colorado did say she saw somebody in the family going to jail for a very long time. She asked if I knew who that might be? When I responded that I have no idea, perhaps she did not want to be the one to break the news to me. I do remember that when she told me my mother was living in New Zealand with a new family and didn't want to be found, it stirred deep unrest in the depths of my soul.

A Poem

12th of November 2002
Colorado, USA,

She Who Seeks Visions

How could I be so sure
And yet, so wrong
Of absolute indecision
But still, I knew all along

Wishing to trade Band-Aids for rainbows
Sorrow for a kiss
A lost and wounded inner child
And succumb her to bliss

A deceit that is no more told as true
The beauty that can be known
As a stone's ripple on the water
Dandelions to the wind, blown

Seek flame, fear not the fire
From the intensity I yield
No longer must I doubt
Thy broken wings shall be healed

As I've said, I loved how free I felt while living and travelling through the US. I remember the moment that my solo delight changed, though. I don't get lonely per se – in fact, the only time I feel fully at peace and most blissful is on my own and in nature – but the pervasive drive to feel fulfilled within a family unit or soul-tribe, and my deep longing to become a mother, was often niggling on the outskirts. The moment that feeling took centre stage was on Christmas Eve in 2004. It was snowing in Colorado. I was living on the road at the time and the heater in my van had just stopped working, so I was fully rugged up, gloves, beanie, blanket across my lap and all while driving. I drove past a house with smoke blowing out the chimney and a warm glow emanating from the windows. A car pulled up in the driveway and the occupants jumped out carrying presents and greeting their friends or family with big, embracing hugs. That moment was a turning point in my travels and maturity. I wasn't enjoying my freedom in the same way I had been. I suddenly wanted to have a family around, to feel loved by others and to have a sense of belonging. I wanted to go home. But I didn't know where that was.

I was living in San Diego in 2008 when Uncle Greg and Auntie Merilyn came to visit, just briefly. They caught me up on family matters and gave me a beautiful bracelet, which was a collective gift from my Mother's three siblings. I've kept this to give to my daughter, along with a couple of things that belonged to my Mother, as it's the closest thing to a family heirloom that I have to pass on.

During our catch-up, I made a passing comment about how they both reminded me of my Uncle Paul and Auntie Marilyn, and Greg visibly grimaced. He was silenced by my auntie before he responded as he would've wanted to. I noted that slightly uncomfortable moment, not really understanding it.

I don't recall discussing the inquest into my Mother's disappearance, or if we did I likely shoved it aside, into my inner too-hard basket. Hopeful for the truth, but still believing she was alive! I didn't comprehend the significance of an inquest. I have so much respect and admiration for my Mother's family, for their dignity and perseverance throughout those forty years and especially for the fact they never spoke badly (or truthfully) about my father to me; they waited until I had formed my own conclusions without their input. It must have been so difficult for them, on every level.

My father and stepmother, S, came to visit me toward the end of 2008, when I was living in Hawaii. It was the first time in about eight and a half years I'd seen them, as I'd been living overseas the whole time. I was a bit nervous to see them, as so often in the past, communication between my stepmother and myself had been triggering and stressful. I think their visit went fairly smoothly, other than her criticising the reggae music I had playing in my car; we did have some good laughs together. I enjoyed showing them many beautiful nature spots and my peaceful little jungle shack. They were invited to dinner with the people whose land I was living on. My stepmother constantly domineered the conversation and spoke over my father. The land owner, Jen, thought my slight lack of enthusiasm at seeing them was due to my stepmother's behaviour – but now I understand it goes way deeper than that.

It was not long after their visit that I was on the phone with a friend of a friend who was kindly giving me a psychic reading free of charge. As always, I asked after my Mother. The lady said she could see a man that she claimed had killed my Mother. 'He looks like a bikie,' she stated. Though to be fair, a lot of men in 1982 could have been mistaken for a bikie. She requested I send her a photo of my dad, so she could see if that was who she saw. I left Maui soon after to return to Australia. I didn't send the photo and subsequently completely forgot about this particular reading because again, I guess I wasn't ready to stir up unresolved trauma and admit the truth. I was living a very happy (in between cycles of depression) and free-spirited existence and I don't blame myself at all for my very effective defence mechanisms. I went back to believing that my Mother was still alive somewhere in the world and that I would find her again one day. Any notion that my father was responsible for her disappearance was shoved down into the murky depths and consequently ignored by my conscious mind.

I left Maui quite abruptly in 2009 as I really wanted to make it back to Australia in time to celebrate my stepsister's engagement party. I'd been dreaming of Australia, and felt like it was time to go back, even though I really didn't want to leave Hawaii. I loved it there. It was the closest I've come to feeling at home on this Earth.

Upon my return, I organised with my sister to surprise the family and she secretly picked me up from the airport without telling anybody. As I approached the waterfront at The Broadwater, my father and his wife were having a picnic on a grassy mound. I walked toward them excitedly and when he saw me, he clenched his chest near his heart, made some guttural gasping sounds and reeled backwards a couple of steps. I joked that I didn't think my return would be that much of a surprise! And we had a laugh. Some years later it occurred to me that I would've been near in age to my Mother the last time he saw her and I more closely resembled her in those days. I had dreadlocks when he'd visited me in Hawaii but had cut them off when I left, so my hair was a similar length to what my Mother's would have been in January of 1982.

Did he think he was seeing a ghost? Or had he forgotten by that time what he'd done and think I was her?

When he looked into my eyes, did he see my Mother's eyes?

CHAPTER SIX

The Truth Hurts...
But Lies Hurt More

The pull I felt to come home and be with my family dissolved when I got back to Queensland. I would often feel confused around my feelings toward my family. I loved them all as individuals and we did have fun and laugh together too, but I never felt a sense of belonging and unconditional love with them. After being away for so long, my feeling of being the misfit only amplified. My father and S had moved back to the Gold Coast and my sister was in Queensland too.

It wasn't long before my family were waving me goodbye once again. We enjoyed a picnic, then exchanged loving goodbyes at Southport Marina, where I was boarding a yacht to sail up to Airlie Beach. I guess my family had become used to my not being around and probably weren't surprised that another adventure had called me to action.

A Diary Entry

March 2009
Queensland

It's so challenging being here with my blood family. I realised I'm trying to create change externally again, and it's causing me angst. I know the only real change that I can progress with is internally. So something I'm pondering, when I leave is it self-preservation? Or is it running away? Do I stay with this pain until it doesn't hurt anymore? Or do I remove myself in order to heal again?

I keep wanting to have heart to hearts with my sister. I want her to let me in. I want to feel loved and accepted by my family. I guess there's a need to love and accept myself a little more. Or maybe they do, and I just can't see it. Sherry thinks I dwell, I think she doesn't deal. Maybe we're both right, but it really doesn't matter who's right and who's wrong. She blames me going away for why we're not close. But there's plenty of people I'm still close with regardless of physical separation. So, what is at the root of this so I can let it go?

I need to move more. She needs to move less and go within. Perhaps it's not my job to help her realise that. I call on the Goddess Kali to help me with strength, determination, and courage.

What is in the highest good?

On the yacht bound for Airlie Beach, there was me, Captain Simon and an English couple. The English woman and I got so, so terribly sick for the first two days on board. The guys were sick too, but they'd vomit and then go and make

98

themselves food, whereas the other woman and I could barely move or talk! I remember when we anchored on land for the first time in those two days, literally kissing the ground and considering living on the island. The following five days were heavenly though, and made up for the first two days of hell. I was extremely grateful when I 'got my sea legs'.

A Dream

27th of March 2009
Queensland

Of Ian (my first real boyfriend), flying with me and holding me, he wrapped his wings across me in a loving embrace and the dream felt really magical.

I wonder if he's passed over …?

The sunrises and sunsets at sea are phenomenal. Of a night, there are so many stars without the light interference from the land. During a night watch travelling up the east coast, we saw phosphorescence and frantically searched for anything dispensable to throw overboard so we could keep the magic glow activated. We saw copious amounts of shooting stars. We stopped at Lady Musgrave Island, where I went on a solo vision quest and perched on a large rock atop a mountain, no other people in sight. I sang songs for the eagles I could see; they then came and circled me on my way down, which felt like a blessing.

Shanelle Dawson

When we anchored out of Middle Percy Island, we swam ashore. On the island we found coconuts and a sailor's 'museum', with random nautical memorabilia and a guest book signed by all sorts of interesting characters. The others complained about my bringing the coconuts back to the boat because there was not much room and I threw all but two back out to sea, but when our desalinisation machine stopped working, who was laughing then?! On another island, there was a treehouse, and the sight of it upon the white sand next to the palm trees, surrounded by aqua clear water, nearly made me cry as it was so close to my dream home.

The trip to Airlie Beach got me hooked on sailing. When we arrived at our destination, I spent the next month volunteering on two of the tall ships in Airlie Beach, sailing around the Whitsundays – so ridiculously beautiful, it doesn't feel real. I was given permission by the owners of one of the ships to sleep on board in between trips. I really enjoyed sleeping on the deck under the stars when no-one else was on board.

A Dream

April 2009
At sea

I'm leaving the family and S says since she gave the others silver rings, she has a gift for me (in real life, S had given both of my sisters gold rings but not me, claiming it was because I don't wear gold, which is true, but I can't help thinking it is more likely because she still didn't like me).

*I think I'm catching a plane; my sister had left a
note on her door. I'm nearly late, but find out that
what I needed to be on time for was a dating service
dad had signed me up for. I refuse to go.*

After a month of starry nights, I went back to living on the
land and started working in a local herb shop in Airlie Beach.
That's where I saw a 'help wanted' sign on a noticeboard. It
was an advertisement for a job working for an adventurous
family as a live-on-board teacher for two boys, aged eight
and ten. I applied for the job and got it. Before I set sail
again, I flew back to the Gold Coast to see family and to
celebrate my and my sister's birthday. It was July 2009.

I was greeted at the Cairns airport by the lovely family,
ready to board the boat which was moored at the marina
and excited to move into my new cabin. The plan was to
head north, then follow the outline of Australia across the
Top End, through the Kimberley then back down the west
coast. Once in Cairns, my belated birthday present to myself
was to go skydiving. The guy who was my tandem diver was
shaking a little as he strapped me into my harness. Not very
reassuring! I made a joke with him, saying, 'Hey, isn't it me
who's supposed to be nervous?' He laughed and asked if it
was that obvious. I joked further saying, 'I'm not afraid to
die, but I don't think today is the day. There's still more I'd
like to do on Earth.' He visibly relaxed as we shared more
banter and we had a great jump together. It felt surreal
to fly. It doesn't feel like you're zooming at 160 kilometres

per hour; it just feels timeless. We had a moment of rain, which stings your exposed skin as though you're being pricked by acupuncture needles, but thankfully we passed through it quickly. The jump doesn't last long; this is why I prefer hang-gliding, which is a slower descent.

Once I reached the ground, I experienced what I now know as adrenal fatigue. I wasn't scared, but my body had been in a fairly constant state of fight or flight for many years, even though I was happily oblivious to the fact. Once back at the skydiving headquarters, I slept for two hours on their couch, unable to move. It was slightly embarrassing but I'm told it happens often!

After setting off on the boat from Cairns, I embraced my new life. I felt honoured to be entrusted with the teaching of the boys and to be welcomed as a part of their lives. The experience was thoroughly enjoyable. When we were docked at a marina, I could come and go as I liked after school and on weekends. But when we were moored on anchor, I found it challenging to be on someone else's timetable, getting a ride to shore and needing to be back at a particular time to return to the boat. There were a few times when we were really remote (one time for about two weeks), where we didn't have much – if any – contact with other people or phone reception, though I didn't mind this at the time. It was a large boat, and I had my own cabin, which was quite luxurious, but also necessary, being in such close quarters with each other for extended periods! I would lie on my bed at times and just watch islands floating by my window. One day I was relaxing on my bed and saw a water snake paddle by! I loved dancing on the deck with my headphones on, doing yoga (very challenging when moving), practising my flute and, at night, more star gazing.

I had the most vivid dreams on the boat.

A Dream

19th of July 2009
Sailing the Whitsundays

Then. I'm watching my dad's mum, Nandi, handing out her kitchenware. She's giving each of us a saucepan and something else from her unit. We realise she's giving away all of her belongings and we were having our last goodbyes.

In late August, while anchored off Lizard Island, I dreamed that my father was telling me about his mother's funeral and I was insisting on being there. A week later, Nandi passed away. I wrote about it in my diary.

A Diary Entry

25th of August 2009

Nandi went back home to spirit yesterday morning. Death is a strange concept for the human mind. I do believe there's just transference of energy. That it's her spirit that animates the body and her spirit lives on outside the body. Nandi, I'll miss our talks. But I'm glad you're at peace and in total love again now.

Shanelle Dawson

A Dream

27ᵗʰ of August 2009
Anchored off Horn Island, Queensland

*I'm angrily yelling at dad to take responsibility
for his choices/actions of the past!*

Somewhere near Darwin, I was with a friend on the boat. My friend didn't consider herself psychic, though she was able to communicate with her mother, who has passed over. I showed her a photo of my Mother. She immediately felt as though she couldn't breathe and that she was being strangled. I must have gone into shock because I don't recall the details very clearly nor did I write about them in my journal at all, which is unusual. What I do recall is that she was able to hear my Mother speaking; and she told her very specific details, such as that it was premeditated and that he used her favourite blue belt. My Mum's friend remembered that favourite blue belt when I relayed this conversation to her.

My friend described the area where my mother was buried near Bayview, but when some members of my family went to the spot and had a scope around, there were lots of rocks, hard ground and a steep slope and they weren't able to do much with that information. Of course, she gave this information to the police, but I'm not sure how seriously they took it. I realise they get a lot of different reports and can't follow them all up, especially from someone claiming to be

104

hearing my Mother telling her. It sounds unbelievable to those who don't believe in that stuff, I know, but if you were there and could hear the details, she wasn't making it up. It must've been so incredibly difficult for her to tell me what she was experiencing, to break that truth to me. I had a lot of resistance to hearing it, especially the part where she felt it was premeditated ... but when my denial couldn't hold me 'safe' anymore, it gave way to the deep inner knowing. I could feel the truth of what she'd shared in my bones. While my head said 'NO', a resonant 'yes' encompassed my whole being. My friend told me she felt a lot of compassion for me in that moment, but she also felt compelled to right the wrongs and honour my Mum.

I believe I've always known this truth and have repressed the memories. It might seem obvious to many others, but those who have known my dad's good side understand the disbelief. All of a sudden, so much made sense – the snapshots of incoherent memories, also the lack of childhood memories, some of those flashes of weird moments I've had with dad, where the cracks have shown, the way my Mother's memory was banished and we never spoke of her, nor had any photos of her, mentioned her birthday or anything about her. Also, what now seemed so clearly linked, my trust issues with men and the type of relationships I had co-created, as well as the stress response my body would have when I saw my father.

On the one hand, my Mother abandonment issues dissolved and the belief returned, to my very core, that my Mother really did love us and would never have left her two beloved daughters and loving family willingly. But on the other hand, now the massive, bloody raw wounding around my father lay exposed and needed tending.

When we reached the Kimberley, my dreams had a waterlogged, gloomy, muddy feel to them. This felt directly connected to all of the crocodile medicine; the pre-historic reptiles were all around and often very close, lurking near the surface – so metaphorical! I needed to get into my murky, internal, sludgy 'eek' and filter it, clean and clear.

A Dream

13ᵗʰ of November 2009
The Kimberley

Of sleeping on the wet concrete ground beside our pool at Bayview. It wasn't fully built yet and my father was inside the empty, concrete shell.

After the realisation, I continued teaching the boys during the weekdays, then would sit with this new reality in private, slowly digesting the truth. I would've been on a bit of autopilot until I could finish up teaching for the year. I watched the film *Peter Pan* in my cabin, remembering one of the two times that I'd seen my father cry. The first time I saw proper tears from him was due to J leaving (and possibly also due to the realisation that he'd murdered our Mum for no good reason, as evident in his comment that he 'wished he'd tried harder to make it work' with her). The second time was when we took K as a young girl to the movies during one of her interim holiday visits. I looked at my dad and saw a tear rolling down his cheek. I thought at the time that what had triggered his sadness was missing out on so much of K's life, but as I sat watching *Peter Pan* again as an adult, it dawned on me … The Lost Boys, who had *no mother*! Was that the slightest sign of remorse …?!

After making it to Broome on the boat, the mum, the boys and I skipped the rough seas of the Indian Ocean and left the dad to navigate the west coast with a friend. From Broome we flew to Perth and stayed in Fremantle, on the southwest coast of Australia. I made the difficult decision not to continue on with the family on the boat after the Christmas holidays. As wonderful as it had been, I could feel the situation had reached completion. The winds of change were wisping around and tugging on my skirts and I was ready to have my full freedom back.

A Dream

4ᵗʰ of December 2009
Perth, Western Australia

Ship docks and salty air.
I awake with the song 'Botany Bay' playing in my
head; haven't heard that since Primary School!

In Perth, I visited my father's sister, my cousin and her family, who live there. We went to see a theatre production of *Sweeny Todd: The Demon Barber of Fleet Street.* I didn't know what we were seeing until we got there. It was a horror musical about a barber killing all of these people. This was not long after my friend told me she'd had a vision of my Mother being strangled to death. It was really intense, confronting and weird. My time in Perth was marked by a distinct feeling of déjà vu.

After finishing work on the boat, I bought a car and decided to drive across to the other side of the country, to the east coast to have Christmas with my family for the first time in nine years. Part of my decision to drive rather than fly was to see more of the country, but mostly to give myself time to integrate what I'd come to know before seeing my father and to help me feel into how I might approach things. Having spent six months on the boat following someone else's plan, it felt great to be on my own schedule again. I love the feeling of being able to choose my own destiny and go where the magic takes me.

A Diary Entry

10th of December 2009

I begin my journey.

Days One and Two

Beautiful, clear, aqua-watered beaches of the lower West Coast,
Cape Naturaliste with its stunning, sweeping ocean views of whales
swimming and with black sand so hot it burns your feet to where it
feels cold, no trees, only shrub brush for shade.

Day Three

I find a waterfall and spot an emu Mama with three chicks.

Days Four and Five

Esperance and Twilight Bay, some of the most beautiful lands I've
seen. The car is starting to overheat now …

Days Six, Seven and Eight

Wild and free dust devils.

I'm now having the adventure of crossing the Nullarbor Plain with
an overheating radiator! I had to drive with the heater on to stop
the engine overheating, in the middle of Summer! A fried engine,
though I don't know if the head gasket was cracked when I bought it,
or if it is occurring as a result of my car protesting the crossing of the
Nullarbor?!

The flies are many and insisting on trying to find moisture in every crevice available to them. It is joked that is why Australians tend to mumble when we talk. I am drinking two litres of water before 9am due to the extreme heat, which has resulted in the best hot chocolate I have ever had ... One whole block gone to liquid and it hasn't cooled enough to re-solidify, even at night.

The stars are so incredibly amazing with no city light interference (like at sea) and the night brings necessary, sweet relief from the oppressive heat!

At one point in the journey, I was listening to the song 'Lies' by The Waifs and I had to pull over to bawl my eyes out. A totally different context, but some of the words struck deep. The song is about being told what you want to hear, closing your eyes and opening your ears, to hear the lies. Lies, lies, all lies! Once I started to see the lies I'd been told, it was hard to see where they ended.

On day nine of my trip, I stopped in at Newcastle to visit my Uncle Greg and Auntie Merilyn. At some point I spoke the words, 'I believe my father murdered my Mum.' They gave me big hugs; there were tears and they expressed so much relief that I had finally come to know the truth.

Greg, Merilyn and my Mum's other two siblings, Phil and Pat, had faced the brutal reality long before I came to understand it. I have a lot of respect for them letting me come to the realisation on my own. It couldn't have been easy for them knowing what they did and seeing us believe otherwise, because we swallowed all of the lies we'd been fed. I can't imagine the amount of tenacity and endurance they had to muster to keep faith that the truth would come out. Every time there was a coronial inquest, they must have gotten their hopes up, only to have them fizzle out when things didn't go any further. After the 2001 inquest that found my father had killed my Mother, another inquest was held in 2003 and once again the coroner recommended that charges be laid against my father. When that recommendation was ignored for the second time, they'd pretty much given up hope, I'm sure.

Uncle Greg pulled out some paperwork he had from the coronial inquests and reading those files was so extremely confronting, but it helped to make it all really sink in, in a very grounded and solid way. Part of me still wanted to believe that it might have been an accident, but that was yet another grasping of hope that my dad might still not be that horrible. The evidence suggested otherwise; and I had to let that hope dissolve along with so much else. It became clear that he'd been having an 'affair' with J, something he always denied … and that there was a lot of other completely inappropriate behaviour going on at his school and at home. This was all new information to me at the time, and rocked me to my core. The father I'd believed in, certainly was no more.

I travelled from Newcastle to Sydney and on days ten and eleven of the journey I visited my Auntie Pat and then Anna (my Mother's friend). While I was in Sydney a friend drove me out to Bayview, where I was wanting to trigger actual rememberings as well as to honour my Mum. I was still in shock and was praying to my Mum for answers.

This was the first time I'd been to Bayview as an adult and since realising my Mother was never coming back.

———

After two weeks on the road, I arrived at the Gold Coast to stay with my sister and spend Christmas with the family.

Seeing my father for the first time since the realisation was as if I was in an unpleasant lucid dream. I felt like I was in an altered state and couldn't relate to anyone in my family, especially my father, in the same way. My father kept telling me I'd lost my sense of humour, but it was more that I simply didn't find him as funny, now that I knew; now I could see that a lot of his jokes were subtle putdowns and I couldn't seem to make myself play along with that part anymore.

I chose not to confront my father right away; I didn't want to ruin everybody else's Christmas Day. My father and S were property managing a villa collective in Runaway Bay on the Gold Coast. They were living in a resort-style house on the grounds. Both of my step-siblings were there too. I remember my stepbrother complaining about his mum and going on and on about it over lunch. My sister and I met eyes across the table and we exchanged a knowing look. 'You've got a mother who loves you. What do you have to complain about? Just fucking appreciate her! And oh, how much we'd love a Mum who loves us!' the glance said. My sister, who doesn't like to talk about such things, said so much in that exchange. I felt a bond with my sister in that moment.

Over Christmas, we were playing a game of family Monopoly, and my father kept ending up in jail. I found it ironic, but there was nobody else present who would get that 'joke'. And I still didn't know if the evidence would ever tip in favour of the law recognising the truth of what he had done.

CHAPTER SEVEN

Exploring Inner and Outer Dimensions

Alongside my words, I also drew pictures in my diaries in my younger years. I've sketched views from my window, created dot therapy artwork to release anger and drawn butterflies, so many butterflies. For me, butterflies represent my Mum, so I drew them for her. I don't consider myself an artist as I don't know any techniques, but I've held onto many of the doodles in my diaries from my travels. Nearly every picture I've done is unfinished. I think that's such a metaphor for who I am. I'm always starting things, but I struggle to finish them.

In 2010, I bought a round-the-world ticket with the money I saved working on the boat and teaching the boys. It had two nights booked in Athens and a return flight from London booked for a year later (though I ended up staying away for two), the rest of the trip was a blank canvas.

A Series of Diary Entries

6th of June 2010
Santorini/Thera, Greek Islands

Climbed the mountain today (at Ancient city ruins of Thera) to sit and meditate at the Shrine of Aphrodite, my favourite goddess. I also meditated in the little cave near the church and a gecko walked across my foot. I've hired a four-wheeler and am loving exploring the island this way. I almost ran off the dirt road when a Greek-God looking, shirtless man stepped out of his barn, and washed his face, then just as I passed on the four-runner, turned to smile at me as though he was from a Levi's ad.

I went to visit the ruins at Akrotiri where there is evidence of an ancient, advanced civilisation that once existed but no human remains have ever been found from these people, so it's a bit of a mystery. Some believe it's linked to Atlantis and matches Plato's descriptions. I meditated on the cliffs by the sea there; I have had a fascination with Atlantis since my late teens.

June 2010
Olympos, Turkey, at The Treehouses

I have met some friends and today we hiked around some ruins here, then later two of us were swimming and my friend remembered she'd left her contacts in (or forgot to put them in?) and swam back to shore briefly. I continued swimming around the rock caves until two men in a tinny (small motorboat) approached. I am feeling a little bit vulnerable; they pass me an ice-cream and then ride off. My friend returns and I'm treading water, eating ice-cream and they're out of sight!

I'm in Cappadocia, Turkey, and there are these magical, mushroom shaped rock formations. I really love the rugs, pottery with intricate paint designs and so many of their handcrafts such as tapestries and leather shoes. I am invited for lots of cups of tea as they are trying to sell me rugs … they don't seem to comprehend that I have no home, nowhere to send it back to. I was looking intently at an informative sign, showing the meanings of the symbols in their weaving and rugs and I have been offered to do an apprenticeship of sorts. There seems to be a lot of sons; I hope they're not trying to find a wife! I sit down beside the grandmother next to the loom and she begins to show me how to weave a small rug. It's my first day and she sees one of my rings, which is a snake, spiralling on my finger. She leaps up and is mortified; her superstitions deem me evil. I am trying unsuccessfully to explain to her, then through the help of a family member, that in my culture, the snake is a good omen — one of transmuting poisons, transformation and shedding old, unwanted skins. She settles down but still looks at me suspiciously. I'm feeling quite awkward and misunderstood, though this isn't a new feeling for me. At the end of the day, I thank them all and inform them that I am going to continue my travels …

I finish my last day in Turkey, in Istanbul, with a Turkish Bath, that feels quite luxurious and it feels a fitting farewell as I set off to Cairo …

1st of July 2010
Cairo, Egypt

I'm on the bus when I realise my directions to my hostel are in English and the driver doesn't recognise where to stop. The whole bus conspires to find me an English speaker; when there are none, a young man calls his friend and relays the required information to the driver. That young man with very little English became my tour guide for a few days. Sometimes I do really silly things when I travel; I can be street wise, sensing danger intuitively but also be incredibly naive in other ways. Perhaps my Mother is like a guardian angel for me and my sister; it is amazing I've never been mugged or anything worse!

I am riding horses with this new friend as the sun sets over the pyramids and the dry, mysterious desert. Later, we walk across a bridge, over the famed Nile and there are some men with a ghetto blaster playing belly dancing type music; they're dressed in sequins and harem pants. I pause momentarily to do a brief shimmy and my friend walks off furiously. He explains to me that because I am a woman walking with him alone, that it would be assumed that I am his wife (we were not even lovers) and that my actions had shamed him. That was more insight into a culture I know very little about … and one that was beautiful and tiresome, simultaneously.

In Dahab, Egypt, I go snorkelling in the Red Sea for my birthday, the 9th of July, and some local Bedouins catch me some fresh fish for a delicious feast. Some days later, with another Aussie friend, we climb Mt Sinai to watch the sunrise, though no bushes spoke to me any more than they normally do of God's law.

My Mother's Eyes

19th of July 2010
Marrakech

It is a classical Moroccan welcome; the train is over three hours late, so when it eventually arrives, it is packed with so many people we can barely move, all these sweaty bodies jammed together in the heat! I'm feeling more and more oppressed as a woman travelling on my own in an Islamic country. The previous countries wore down my strength a little in that regard. I was getting harassed on the street, and in the markets. The snake charmer put his finger down my top, to which I declared, 'Haram!' Forbidden. His eyes were as black as the cobra he was luring out of the basket, but the intensity of the danger is somewhat alluring.

I was trying on a piece of clothing at a market stall and when I stepped out of the change room to look in the only mirror, the man running the stall stood behind me and rubbed himself up against me. When I jumped aside and shot him a glaring look, he went straight to denial. 'What, what? I didn't do anything,' he said. The fight response was heightened and constant in me by this time. I started to question my own mental health and knew I needed to go somewhere I felt safer, where my nervous system could relax.

It was such a massive relief to board a ferry across to Spain, stepping onto lands where I could wear what I wanted again without having to cover my body in the heat, and where men were flirtatious but not infiltrating and disrespecting of my boundaries. Some locals I met told me of a bit of a community they thought I'd love called 'Corazon Verde' (Green Heart) in Ibiza, so after some other wonderful Spanish experiences, I travel across land and sea to visit. I naively knew nothing of the party culture of the island, *nor did I engage in it, but I have a wonderful time working on the land and meeting lovely Earth-loving people; music, markets, massages, the cobalt blue Mediterranean.*

For almost a decade, I carried around the set of instructions to get to the intentional community in the Canary Islands. These were the directions given to me by a guy in a hostel in Florida, with the hope it could be home, or at the very least an adventure. I had, with a sliver of intrigue, inscribed these directions from diary to each new diary throughout those years. I don't recall what year I was reading *High Tide in Tucson* by Barbara Kingsolver, where in the book she feels compelled to visit the Canary Islands and, in particular, La Gomera. I believed it was a sign when she is outlining and describing her journey just as I've mapped it in my imagination numerous times, waiting for the time to feel right to visit. In the book, she didn't however go to the community I was recommended, but her captivating description of the island only gave impetus to my intrigue, and I knew I would one day follow those instructions. That day had finally arrived ...

On the ferry there, I met an older local guy who invited me to stay with him in his spare room. Through him, I met an English woman named Hannah who I became good friends with and who eventually hired me as a nanny to look after her daughter while the father of the girl was away. I lived in their separate little mud brick adobe studio just down the path from their home. I love La Gomera; it is this really fascinating mix of beautiful, looming green mountains, cascading into green velvet, terraced valleys, but instead of lush rainforest there are cacti, palm trees and rich clay which feeds their pottery. The black volcanic rock which lines some of the beaches has sparkling peridot in it (a green stone called olivina by the locals) and makes the Mediterranean a deep, sapphire blue. La Gomera is predominantly Spanish-speaking, though the natives had their own language before the Spanish invaded and colonised the islands. It is said that they used to communicate through whistles, which carry nuances better than shouting across the valleys. They were a farming and sheep-herding people, not into boating, which is unusual on an island. There's a site atop a mountain called a lagoon, with no water in sight. It makes me wonder what these lands once looked like and if there is a connection to Atlantis or Lemuria (another possible ancient, advanced civilisation), as some people believe.

While I was on the island, I did eventually make it out across the valley to the community I'd been told about. It was amazing to finally arrive at the place I'd carried with me for so long. Once I got there, although it was very beautiful, I realised it wasn't quite what I was looking for. I've been told it has become quite commercialised since that person would've visited a decade earlier. I did, however, sleep in some nearby caves and on some rocks by the sea, inviting the mysteries of the stars to shine their light on my path.

I don't travel with a phone or laptop, so I was only able to send and receive messages to people back home on rare visits to an internet cafe. I know I wasn't very good at staying in touch with my family, or anybody really. I liked to think it was because I lived in the present. I relate best to what's right in front of me. But it could also have been because I was still in denial and trying to avoid heartache.

The messages I did exchange with my family were light-hearted. It's difficult to read back on emails and messages with my father now. Our conversations are full of banter, cheeky humour and laughs. I miss them. I miss him. It's confusing to miss certain parts of my father, while also detesting him for others.

Back in Australia, my stepsister was preparing for her wedding. I didn't go because I was scared I would explode at my father and destroy her day. I drove around the whole island of La Gomera, to all four of the main villages to find an appropriate wedding gift, but didn't. I'm sure they perceived this as lack of care or thoughtfulness, but it wasn't; I genuinely shopped all day trying to find something … and I can't stand shopping!

A Dream

23rd of August 2010
La Gomera

Of a green, deserted botanical garden with ornate chairs. There's a huge glass window and I can see two knights jousting, full Renaissance style.

122

Of horse-drawn carriages, back in time and musty, old,
haunted theatre buildings, hearing footsteps creaking up the stairs.

(It would seem this was Glastonbury
calling me, though I didn't know it yet.)

While living in the Canary Islands, I called my half-sister K on the only number I had for her. It was a number from when K was still living at home with her mother. I was shocked when J answered my call. I was expecting K's voice, not J's, and it was confronting to suddenly find my ex-stepmother on the other end of the phone.

On the call, I told her that I'd come to realise some of the reasons she'd reacted the way she had to my sister and me, and I did tell her I'd forgiven her, but I realised afterward that I hadn't fully.

'Oh, it was a horrible, horrible time,' she said. And that was all. That was all from the woman who as a girl had 'replaced' my Mother. I thought she might have acknowledged how hard it was for us, but she didn't.

At some point, J did write my sister and me a letter, but our half-sister who'd been entrusted with the delivery, out of loyalty to her mother, chose not to give it to us. I *really* wish I could've read that letter; I feel it would've been very helpful to my sister and myself along our healing path and in undoing some of the damage caused.

The phone call was the first – and only – contact I had with J since she left us. It was an unsettling experience.

A Dream

I'm with my three cousins and my sister; there are all of these caravans or dwellings. My cousin won't look me in the eye, so I ask if she's still mad at me. My other cousin was encouraging her sister to say what she wanted to say to me, and my sister started to cry. I ask her how they would've acted if she were me?

In early November 2010, my friend Hannah was heading back to her Motherland, England, for a wedding, so one of our friends and I decided to go with her. I brought all of my things with me (not that I had a lot), and I felt a strange sense of grief at leaving, considering my intention was to return with them both. The three of us had a lovely time together. There were a lot of laughs, like when we attempted to learn how to sing 'Happy Birthday' in Slovenian for our friend, to help her with her homesickness.

After we visited Stonehenge for the first time, I couldn't talk afterward for a few hours! I don't know why, but the energy there had such a strong effect on me … magnetic. I was getting the sense that I needed to remain in England, so I turned to my friends and I told them I was going to stay. 'I know this is completely insane, but I don't feel like I'm meant to come back to the Canary Islands with you. I feel like I'm meant to stay here,' I said.

I waved them off at the airport with some tearful goodbyes and went and hired a car. I purchased a map and circled a couple of spots where I felt energy. The place that had the most energy for me was Glastonbury. But before I made it there, I had the most amazing (and freezing fricken' cold!) adventure, visiting Sherwood Forest, the Lakes District, the stunning Scottish Highlands and another place I'd always wanted to visit called 'Findhorn'. I was chasing rainbows all day as I drove to this truly magical community, where they once defied the laws of physics, working with the elementals of the lands and growing phenomenally sized vegetables. That's how I ended up in the historic Somerset town of Glastonbury in the southwest of England.

In my early days there, I stayed in a hostel before I moved into a house with a few other women at the foot of the Tor, and all its rich goddess history. It is such a beautiful and powerful area, and it felt incredibly familiar to me, like I'd been there before. One of the many riches of the area, as well as 1000-year-old yew trees, was the way that many of the gatherings were a harmonious merging of pagan and Christian celebrations. There is a Goddess Temple and much reverence for the Goddess in all of her forms, but also the strong Jesus/Mary influence. Joseph of Arimathea (the man who buried Jesus after his crucifixion in the Bible) had planted a cutting of a holy thorn on a hill in Avalon/ Glastonbury. I was living there when someone cut down the tree. I mourned with the local community as we tied ribbons and sang songs together, and circled around the remains of the sacred tree.

I remember the first time I met Peter. It was fairly soon after I arrived in Glastonbury. I was walking home from town in the early evening and ran into a woman who I'd met earlier at the library. She introduced me to her roommate. They'd just been at a meditation and Peter was jumping all around because he was freezing, so it was only a brief interlude, but he started appearing in my dreams, which I thought was strange given we'd only just met. The second time we saw each other was at the Chalice Well at the Winter's Solstice ceremony. We sat on a wooden bench among the pan-like gardens, looking up to the Tor, and shared some beautiful moments. Our first date, we went to a nearby town and participated in Dances of Universal Peace, which was so endearing and lovely.

Peter was a very beautiful person, but he also had extremely strong defence mechanisms which I saw straight through, and he had a lot of fear. Our soul connection was deep, but the human part was complicated. We would appear in each other's dreams and several times found ourselves in the same nature spot, or with a favourite tree, simultaneously. He accused me of putting a spell on him, which I would never do, but I was under it too.

Two years previously, Peter's girlfriend had broken his heart when she left him to return to New Zealand and he stated that it had taken him those two years to recover, so he was resistant to fall in love again, and he was convinced I would leave too and that his mental health couldn't cope with that. There was a constant push and pull, which has been an unhealthy pattern in all of my relationships and one I understand now I'm aware of attachment styles. It may be perceived as weak that I stayed in this dynamic, but it actually felt to me as though it was my strength that kept me there. I could tell he had mental health issues, and I was faced with a question I'd asked myself before in relationships: how much do you allow someone to 'get away with' in understanding what is out of their control and due to illness? It seems to me, sometimes you have to deeply dive into patterns to really see them for what they are, to know them fully in order to change them.

On Peter's birthday, the 8th of March, I put together a package with all of his favourite foods and went to his house to drop it off. He wasn't home, though his roommate let me in and I left the package outside his bedroom door and went home. I couldn't sleep. I felt like an anxious mother dog that couldn't get to her puppies. I was having a panic attack, but I didn't understand what it was about. When Peter came to visit me the next day, he confided in me that he'd been suicidal and had gone to the forest with the intent of not coming back out. Instinctively I felt that, but I didn't know how to interpret those feelings.

Living in Glastonbury, I was babysitting a gorgeous little girl, as well as doing some caregiving work for an older man. I found and bought my medicine drum and we had lots of drumming circles, sweat lodges, meditations, breath work sessions, kirtans, ceremonies … Life was saturated with goodness in so many ways. And still, my past remained.

I received an email from my father while I was in England. He encouraged me to go to Cornwall, which was nearby, and where an *Antiques Roadshow* episode had been filmed. One of the supposed sightings of my Mother happened in that episode. A woman in the audience had looked like Mum, and my father suggested I go to Cornwall to see if I could find the woman in the footage. I was livid. I sent a furious email to my Mother's brother ranting about how heartless it was for my father to string his own daughter along like that. It was cruel of him to give me any kind of false hope.

En route, I did end up going to Cornwall and I have a photo of the church there. Even though I didn't believe my Mother was alive at that point, there was still a tiny part of me keeping hope. What if she was? What if the woman in the crowd was her? What if I ran into her on the street? I couldn't help but search for her face. I know that might sound delusional, but denial is a common reaction to trauma.

A Dream

4th of March 2011
Glastonbury, England

Of the Dawson family, my uncle and cousin very strongly, very toxic emotions. And a muddy obstacle course.

Peter and I danced that complicated dance for about a year overall, though at some point I decided to travel to Ireland with the desire of breaking the unhealthy patterns. I harboured the hope that if the situation was given some proper space and Peter had time for reflection, then when I returned he might be ready for a more solid relationship with me. Peter was regularly in my dreams, and I was deeply sad. As much as I wanted to be with him, I knew we could only be together if our connection could evolve to a healthier version of what we were sharing.

A Diary Entry

April 2011
Woof-ing (Working On Organic Farms), Ballina,
Northwest Coast of Ireland

It's a Full Moon and I'm having lots of triggers. I recognised the little girl inside of me, who tried so hard to be 'good', to work hard and her efforts weren't appreciated or praised. Adult me held her and thanked her. As I lay by the cold sea on a six-ft high, circular mound of dirt and bright green grass, I am surrounded by tufts of scented flowers, a hare hopped close by. He seemed curious to see me, stayed looking for some moments then, not sure what to make of me he hopped away and as he did, a blue heron squawked loudly as it flew directly overhead.

I was back in Glastonbury in time to dance the Maypole for Beltane. When the dynamic between Peter and myself didn't

129

improve, in August of 2011 I accompanied my roommate to an ashram in France to help her with her transition to her new home there. I thought what we were arriving to was a quiet mountain stream community of four people, to work hard on the lands and get some reflection time. But my friend neglected to mention that there would be a kundalini yoga retreat for forty-five people, which entailed 4.30 am starts, lots of food prep and cold showers! Once the retreat was over, I joined another three people to drive across the French Alps to Italy, where we stayed in a community called 'Damanhur'. It was a very unusual place – albeit quite fascinating – with these amazing mosaic art cathedral caves, which the founding residents began digging into the rocks with hand tools in the 70s. I really loved a lot about this community but again, it didn't feel like home to me, so I continued on my journey.

In the picturesque Italian villages on the Cinque Terre hiking trail, I marvelled at the vineyards, sweeping coastal views and some beautiful ruins built in 1106, including the church of Saint Peter, as well as a boat named *Pietre*. I realise Peter is a common name, but I started seeing it everywhere and that wasn't helping me to let him go! I sat by the grotto that was the inspiration for some of Lord Byron's poetry, with my pen and journal in hand. There were stunning cliffs and caves, where people jumped into the beautiful, cerulean blue water. Sleeping in the airport in Milano one night, to choose where in the world to go, I decided to go to a gathering in Portugal. I emailed Peter a goodbye of sorts, though I continued to see the name Pedro everywhere. At the bus stop, waiting to head north, a lady with her grandson arrived to wait for the same bus. He was blond with bright, blue eyes and looked like a young version of Peter. After a bit of chatter, I discover his name is … Peter! On the bus, in among the Portuguese music, the song 'Vincent' by Don McLean started playing and I hid my face in the corner of the window as my eyes rained tears. I love this song and it reminded me so much of Peter.

A Diary Entry

7ᵗʰ of September, 2011
Portugal

Preparing to sleep outside in a lovely spot under some trees on the outskirts of the village, overlooking a lake with the sound of church bells chiming. I realise it's too cold to sleep outside in these mountains on the damp earth, so I'm calling it a mini vision quest and doing midnight yoga instead as I drift in and out of sleep. I like being awake when the access to the vision of stars dissolves, the birds weave their dance above my head to alight my heart, and the hues of the rising sun give hope to my soul.

A Dream

September 2011
Vila Boa, Portugal

Otherworldy! Beautiful medieval, priestess vibes, Avalon. I'm told I'm going back (to Glastonbury) for one last 'clearing' ceremony before I can go and live anywhere in the world I want. I turn the light on a small fish aquarium clock, it was Peter's and he comes to inform me it's the wrong time.

A Series of Diary Entries

10th of September 2011
Near Salto, Portugal

Today I walked about ten or eleven hours. At one point I came across a band of wild horses, wow! Their unfathomable energy was so boundless, wild and free … so captivatingly beautiful! I was rendered speechless and in complete awe of their majesty. My maternal instincts were awakened by the foals with velveteen fur as they clung to their mamas' sides and by the calves I saw earlier, with their large eyes of pure innocence.

18th of September 2011

The Mayor in the nearby village of Salto has given a house to us travellers for the winter (and possibly longer), because too many of their young people have moved away and they need more youthful, competent energy to contribute to the village here. I'm helping clean, though I am feeling the winds of change and intend on moving on. They have a monthly fiesta, which we are invited to. So, with our plates of shared food, we arrive and dance and feast and laugh together, it is a beautiful occasion.

25th of September 2011
Near Ourense, Northwestern Spain

I realised it's the 25th today, my Mum's birthday, hopefully I can get to the sea to drum and sing for her. We are on a girls' road trip, on our way to some hot springs, then the others will go to find some grape picking work. I find it exhausting travelling with other people and intend on hiking some of the Camino (Santiago de Compostela). Oh my goodness, hilarious! I had a typical Shanelle moment, where I don't plan or research anything properly, gazed at a map whilst looking over someone's shoulder and off I went … I was walking through the town and came to the headquarters where people were receiving certificates and taking photos in proud triumph of their achievements, having FINISHED hiking the trail! I see them, then realise what I've done … caught the train to the end of The Camino … oh dear…!

10th of October
Holland, Netherlands

I love it here. We went to see Amma (the Indian hugging saint) and to a particular forest where the witches would gather, I then went on a mission to find a windmill, which aren't as numerous as one might think …

A new friend has a bad back and needs some help driving to Glastonbury, also with setting up her stall at 'The Fairy Festival'. It seems I am returning after being away for several months. I am *both excited and nervous to see Peter again. At the festival, I am intrigued to meet Josephine Wall, my all-time favourite artist! She is an interesting character and I can see how her personality fits the beautiful fantasy art that she does.*

My connection with Peter has changed, I feel more detached and he isn't letting down his walls much at all either.

There's a photo of Peter and me that reminds me so much of a photo I have of my Mother and father. In it, I'm looking up adoringly at Peter, mirroring the way my Mother looks at my father. Being with Peter made me understand my Mother more, in a way. It's easy to say 'Why didn't you just leave?' to someone in an unhealthy or volatile relationship. But the reality is far more complicated.

Not long after I returned, Peter left Glastonbury to travel on the 10th of November 2011. It was a full moon in Glastonbury. We'd spoken about travelling together, but I could feel it was a journey he needed to do alone. Peter wanted to go and get healing for his mental health. Having tried Western medicine approaches to no avail, he went in search of medicine people.

A Diary Entry

10th of November 2011
Glastonbury, England

This morning as Peter left, we said our goodbyes, neither of us knowing how long we were saying goodbye for, nor did I know where he was going. I am deeply sad. It did make me laugh as he texted me from town having just left my side, because it was so typically Peter; he'd missed his bus because he'd been waiting on the wrong side of the road. A person had told him he was on the wrong side and he didn't believe them ... Then he saw a fox. The fox is one of Peter's spirit animals. This was my last memory of him as he went off into the world and I stayed in Glastonbury.

I wouldn't admit to myself that I was staying in Glastonbury waiting for Peter to get back. A week after he left, I dreamed of him. He came and sat beside me in a form I've never seen before, very blue and yellow and magical. He said, 'We've got one more thing to do together,' and we sat on the edge of a cliff and watched the sunset side by side. On the 4th of December, I dreamt of Peter back from his travels, he said he'd been in South America, though in real life I didn't know where he was.

Toward the end of the year, my roommate and I were heading off to the annual Frost Fayre in High Street and I can't explain what happened in detail as I've actually never felt anything like it before and haven't really got words to encapsulate the experience. Just before we walked out the door, a sudden wave of despair hit me so hard I couldn't stand. I lay on the cold, tiled floor in our kitchen and let out an almost involuntary primal wail from depths I didn't know existed in me. My roommate was a bit freaked out; she bent down and kissed the top of my head and left me to it. I was a bit freaked out too, but had learned over the years to trust the process (usually in private, but this had hit me so compellingly and unexpectedly). An hour or two later, I went down to the Fayre but I felt really strange and hadn't identified what it was that had moved through me.

A Dream

16th of December 2011
Glastonbury, England

Of a multi-tiered, beautiful altar. I'm enjoying watching the movie of my life, but someone tells me it's about to turn into a horror movie so I turn it off.

A Diary Entry

21st of December, 2011
Glastonbury, England

We're celebrating the Winter Solstice at the Chalice Well, I feel a little sad and miss Peter as I remember the beautiful moments the year before when he and I first connected. This is one of Lindie Lila's chants we sang at The White Springs today:

Born of Water
Cleansing Powerful
Healing Changing
I am

I decided I couldn't wait for Peter anymore, so I went into my round-the-world ticket and booked a flight to Brazil, via the Canary Islands where I planned to get more work and save up some more money. I was working in England but the cost of living was so high I wasn't saving any money. I tried my hand at apple picking, in the cold rain, perched upon a ladder in layers of thick, winter clothing; I was so slow and even though I was trying my hardest, I only made 12 pounds for a few hours of work! Only a few days after booking my flights, Peter's roommate got a postcard from him that was stamped in Brazil. It seemed like such a synchronicity that I went into a bit of a fantasy in my mind, that I'd go to Brazil and Peter would be there and he would be ready for a proper relationship, and we'd find a community and be together.

A Diary Entry

25th of December, 2011
Glastonbury, England

It is Christmas Day. I went with three of my roommates to visit the 1000-year-old Yew Tree and the Witches Hill — this was a spot Peter and I had visited together and shared a picnic, deep conversation and our hearts. I'm hoping he might return before I leave, so I can say goodbye.

Two days before my flight to the Canary Islands, I had a lovely little farewell at our house in Glastonbury and packed my things once again. The day before my flight, Peter's sister called me. 'Are you sitting down?' she asked me. 'I'm so, so sorry, Shanelle, but Peter's been found dead.'

We both just cried together, united in our grief, for what felt like a long time before I managed to get a few details. I felt like I was swimming in an abyss, trying to grasp for something solid but finding nothing. My heart was shattered into unrecognisable shards.

I broke the news to my roommates, who had known and loved Peter for many years. They cancelled the person who they had lined up to move into my room and I cancelled my flights. I needed to stay and grieve with the people who love and knew him too. I wanted to honour his passing properly and with our mutual friends. I can't explain the feeling of my heart being ripped open … it is comparable to childbirth-raw, bloody, primal and excruciating.

We tried to piece the story together through broken English, from the middle of the jungle to the British embassy in another part of Brazil, to Peter's parents, his sister, then on to me. Peter had been camping in Barcelos in the Brazilian Amazon. His hammock was strung up between two trees and he was making porridge. They found his body, half fallen out of his hammock and face down in the rising body of water which ran alongside his chosen camping spot. At first, they thought it was murder. However, there would be a few variations on the details, lost in translation. His father is a doctor and he would later fly with Peter's sister to Barcelos to help with the autopsy.

Consequently, the official finding was that he'd been stung by an insect and went into anaphylactic shock. It was a bittersweet irony as I recalled a conversation with Peter where he'd said he wanted to die by a wild animal. I assume he'd been referring to a bear or lion type of species and I recall I felt a quiet sadness at the time.

A Dream

30ᵗʰ of December 2011
Staying the night at Peter's sister's house

Of a big, white tent and lots of people and families. A man has parked his car in the meadow nearby, saying it's for a quick getaway and he knows which road to take, to cross the bridge. As he points, I assume the bridge is crossing to an island but then realise it's going across the ocean and into the sky.

Grief is such an intense and organic process; each person must find their best way (or not!) to navigate through its treacherous, densely painful waters. I can't even begin to describe the depth of the emotions I felt after Peter's death. It was as though the sensation went to the very moment my soul was conceived and the movement of those ripples was almost more intense than my physical being could handle. I felt nauseous, and toxic in my emotions. Blah! I couldn't stand well-meaning people saying, 'Don't worry, he's in a better place now.' It made me want to fucking scream. 'I know he's in a better place! I'm angry he's there and I'm stuck here! I'm not grieving for him,

I'm grieving for myself and the finite physical senses that will never experience him again,' I wanted to yell. I felt like a poisonous snake hissing and spitting venom on the inside, numb and subdued on the outside.

I felt angry at the whole world and at Our Creator. As I started to write in my journal, I felt a profound tingling in my right side of my crown and 5D colours, vivid sensations. It felt like Peter in Spirit and it was truly beautiful, but it made me want to go where he was, to escape the emotional pain. Then I remembered when I was fourteen and had a near-death experience and stated clearly, 'I haven't done what I came here to do.' So I knew I had to stay, here on Earth. Had Peter done what he came to do?

In a dream Peter came to me and told me that his determined cause of death was wrong.

On New Year's Eve we had a beautiful memorial for Peter at our local ashram, one place that Peter had lived when he first arrived to Glastonbury and frequented regularly. His sister, with a lot of help, designed various stations with different crafts to create in Peter's honour. We sat in a ceremonial circle and shared stories, feelings, and whatever needed to be witnessed and expressed. I met Peter's mum who had travelled from another part of England. It was really special, though obviously heartbreaking … she was so much in her grace and acknowledged how difficult it was for me. Here she was, having just lost her son, and she was acknowledging how hard it was for me. When I couldn't find the words to match the enormity of what I felt, or to acknowledge what she might feel, we shared a moment looking into each other's eyes, and a warm embrace which spoke more coherently than words.

My beautiful friend Alannah came to support me at the memorial. She wrapped her arms around me tightly and held me as I cried unapologetically. Because I hadn't had a mother figure to hold me like that, I wasn't used to it at times of grief and deep vulnerability. As a kid, I'd give my dad a quick goodnight hug at bedtime, but it wasn't an affectionate, nurturing embrace. It was a formality. Obviously I've had intimacy with beloved's, but this was different. So when Alannah wrapped her arms around me, my first instinct was to push her away, but I surrendered into it. I can still remember the permeating feeling of being held so intimately while I cried in such a raw state.

We sang songs, mostly Indian chants (bhajans) which were an integral part of Peter's life and speak to his soul from his travels to India, but we also sang Earth songs. This is one major gift Peter has given me. Before his death, I sang only on my own in nature or in a small circle of women. His death put so many things into a different perspective for me (as death often does), and I saw how clearly the ego protects us, but also can keep us hiding ... I decided, in his honour and upon invitation, to lead a couple of the songs. Who fucking cares if I hit a bad note or fall flat on my face; it really doesn't matter. I sang loud, strong and uninhibited, like a lioness howling out her grief to the wind. Peter's sister sang the last song; she has such an incredibly beautiful and powerful voice, and her grief only made her song expand further into those most tender places within. All of us joining our voices in unity was profound. Surrounding the altar, created in Peter's honour, were photos of his life. I recognised this altar from the dream I had.

For closing, Peter's sister handed out small 'medicine bundles', sections of his shirt she had cut up to contain some of his copal he liked to burn and some precious strands of his beard. I was holding this bundle in my hands and heart and remembering the feeling of caressing his wiry, red beard, those little curls at the base of his neck and the velvet, downy hair on his ear lobes.

Peter once told me the only time he felt truly alive was when he was with me. In the moment, it was a compliment, but I'm certain he felt resentment toward me for this at times. I like to believe that in the last leg of his journey here on Earth, with the freedom of travel and being in the largest, thriving forest on the planet, that he felt truly alive within his own right before leaving this world.

In one of our last moments together, Peter and I went to a Five Rhythms free-form dance session. I wanted to stop and watch Peter. He moved so intricately and freely. In day-to-day life, he could be quite abrasive and stiff. But when he danced, his expression came from deep within and from his heart with such beauty. Even though I wanted to see Peter in his element, I forced myself to focus on my own experience, as we were meant to. After he passed, I reflected on that moment and wrote Peter a note in the dark ...

I couldn't watch you dance
Or the rest of the world would cease to exist
If I'd known it was the last dance
I would have stared
And let the rest of the world disappear

I stayed and grieved in Glastonbury for about a month. I felt too broken to continue on my adventure and reinstated my flight back to Australia; I felt as though I was returning completely defeated. Little did I know the battles I was about to re-enter into ...

CHAPTER EIGHT

Oceans of Tears

When I first landed back in Australia, I stayed with my sister on the Gold Coast for about a month while I tried to lug my grieving heart into the next chapter of my life. I worked with my father during this time, doing some gardening and maintenance around the complex where he and S were live-in managers. Sleeping in one of my sister's spare bedrooms, I dreamt of my father; he's crying and saying he's sorry.

I was going through the motions on the outside, but inside I was like a pressure cooker, trying to function, while carrying this wide open, deep wound that needed addressing and healing. It was as if Peter's death blew apart all of my defence mechanisms that had held my sanity together and my Mother/father grief largely at bay. This was an extremely difficult 'dark night of the soul' to navigate through and for the next two years it would feel as though life and love as I knew it, had completely crumbled and dissolved in chaotic ruins and disarray. During this time, I escaped to the beach. I'd walk along the shoreline for hours on end. I'd yell out to sea, throw rocks at the horizon, and scream underwater. It would be some time before I could eventually create some semblance of at least momentary fluid order in my life again.

It's at this point I feel like I should admit that I have been suicidal at different times in my life. The thing that brought me back from the edge and stopped me from acting on my thoughts was knowing the harm it would cause my sister and my Mum's family. I didn't want to cause them more grief, sorrow and pain. I didn't want to traumatise anyone. I didn't want someone to have to find my body, and I also didn't want to not leave a body because I know how it feels for loved ones not to have closure.

Over the years, I have tried so many forms of healing modalities. I've seen various psychologists and put concentrated effort into my own healing. At some point, I realised talk therapy wasn't working for me anymore; it was keeping me stuck in the trauma. I can see the value of speaking to a professional – and encourage people who need help to seek it – but there's only so much talking can do. In addition to counselling, I've also participated in family constellations, somatic experiencing, inner child work, various meditation techniques, art therapy, self-prescribed nature therapy, positive affirmations and yoga, among many other things.

Despite years of inner exploration, I haven't found a 'cure', no single treatment has 'fixed' me, though they've all peeled away at the density inside me. With self-awareness and education around trauma and its affects, comes understanding. There's a power in allowing yourself to just be and feel what is authentically there as it arises.

A Diary Entry

26th of February
Gold Coast, Queensland

I'm finding it difficult to relate to this world.

Tomorrow going back to uni to see how I will be able to finish my degree. I feel like I'm faking it all the time, my jaw is always clenched. I feel impatient to move forward with my life, there is too much to feel. I welcome stillness in order to delve deeply, and am trying to find a balance of being and doing.

I feel myself lingering on the edge of a pool of schizophrenia and sometimes I do dip my foot in. I feel my face change to a mask of ugliness and my fragmented selves floating too far apart to merge into one, an abstract jigsaw puzzle begging to fit together but unable to at this time.

My heart is crushed under a tonne of weight and twisted into a mangled wreck.

So much to heal, it feels impossible. My idealistic visions and hopes of the world, smashed and tainted. Great spirit, I want to feel you again.

I'm certain my father knows that I know he did it, because I confided in my cousin who I thought I could trust just before I travelled overseas. I told her about my psychic reading, of how I believed it was my father that killed my Mother, as well as who the psychic told me had sexually abused me (more blocked memories, but undeniable symptoms and flashbacks). She [told] her sisters, who in turn told their parents and then my father. It appears my father, being the extremely manipulative narcissist that he may just be, cunningly poisoned my siblings against me in preparation for the moment I might reveal him.

Upon my return to Australia, something just felt off. Moments of uncomfortable silence, obvious disparities in equality, subtle disdain in the way they treated me, which was screamingly obvious. I knew their projections on to me and perceptions of me were not accurate and this felt confusing and unjust, but I didn't quite put my finger on why this was all occurring at the time. At this point, there didn't appear to be anything happening with the case or of any new evidence against him, so the longing for finding answers were just glimmers of hope and I'm fairly certain some of my Mum's family had almost given up hope at this point, after so many years of waiting for justice.

After my stay at my sister's place, I moved back to the Byron Shire in New South Wales where I had spent some time in 2009. I was trying to start again, while also dealing with the fallout of 'the realisation'. I wrote multiple letters to my father, none of which his eyes have seen. While I tried to determine the best way to sever ties with him, I stayed in the tortuous dance of pretence and each time I saw him, I would fall apart and become a complete mess again, sometimes for weeks afterward.

A Diary Entry

September 2012
New South Wales

If I sleep now, will I wake up from this putrid nightmare? Putrid. That's a word used against me as a child. Useless. That was me. Stupid. An idiot.

I'm a fucking mess right now.

Strung out.

Can't sleep. At least my head has slowed down. The circus is over for now. I feel sick. Is my heart too broken to ever heal?

I woke up the morning after an emotional storm; instead of being grateful to be alive, I wished the storm had gathered me up and taken me away with it. Pathetic. Another word used to describe me when I was younger. Small parts of me still believe that voice from the past, no matter how much I want to let it go. And the bigger parts that don't believe that, want to redesign the parts that are influenced internally by the words.

Good, let the tears come and let them go and take with them all that they can carry. Release.

Crying is beautiful. Not something to be stopped, shamed or seen as weak. It takes strength and honesty to see and work with what's really there without becoming bogged down and stuck in it.

A Diary Entry

11th of October 2012
New South Wales

I feel sick at the moment, sick with toxic emotions so I'm writing to vent and to try and understand my role, my responsibility, my learning in all of this. Quite frankly this whole Earth journey is just too hard. Is my father fucking with my head with more guilt and manipulation or is this something I really do need to look at? Have I really caused my uncle and his family pain? And have I really been so self-centred and selfish since I was seventeen?

My grandmother, Beautiful Nanna, taught me the power of the word hate. I ceased using the word for the next twenty years, until now. There are parts of me that H A T E my father. There are parts of me that have compassion for his suffering and can access unconditional love, but right now his text has triggered so much rage, anger, hurt and resentment that I feel sick.

I'm trying to stay connected to the Source, in light, so I can see the truth of this. I want to disappear from his life. If it wasn't for my sister, I would. He hasn't earned respect and though everyone deserves loving kindness, having him in my life fucks severely with my head and prolongs my suffering. Do I make the choice to cut him out? There are parts of me as crazy as it seems, still clinging to the hope that he didn't do it ... and I could be causing unnecessary suffering for those I love.

But I'm quite certain he did. My cells and bones know the truth of the story of this body and what it remembers. What is my spiritual truth in all of this? We are all fragments of the Divine but if it's unhealthy for me to have him in my life, do I take the opportunity to work with the triggers until I'm no longer triggered, to go deeper into love and compassion for everything, or is the opportunity being presented to love myself more gently and fully to choose not to experience the harshness of being constantly re-traumatised? Is the harshness a normal part of human experience? I was reflecting on this by looking at nature's mirror — or is she at times harsh as a direct result of how humans are behaving? Beauty and the beast? The 3D polarity experience?

I feel the pressure in my head. The crazy head, the hard mask over my face. I guess it's the post-traumatic stress disorder, but I feel autistic. Weird relationship with time and space and colours and senses, writing feels weird.

The memories of the night my Mother disappeared still come back to me in abstract pieces: the front door, my teddy bear, the rain. I believe that I have more repressed memories of that hellish night. I can feel where my conscious mind can only perceive a black void, that there are pieces of the puzzle locked away somewhere in my body, in my mind. Our innate wisdom is so vivid and alive but we, as a culture, have become numb and desensitised to the language of it.

I need those memories out for necessary resolution and much-needed answers to too many questions that won't go away. I want them out of my body. I want to redeem functionality again; it's hard to heal something that's hiding but still very loud. The detective who had reopened my Mother's case had an interest in my memories too. Detective Damian Loone first contacted me through my Auntie Pat, to see if I would be open to meeting with and speaking to him. Although I struggled with the feeling that I was 'betraying' my father and that side of the family, I knew I needed to honour my Mother by doing so.

On the 12th of November 2012, Damian came to Mullumbimby to meet with me. Auntie Pat, Uncle Greg and Auntie Merilyn came up to be a part of the meeting and to offer me support. I actually don't remember much of the conversation; I do recall at one point I mentioned that my lucky numbers are 421 and 214. Damian looked somewhat startled and gestured toward the keyring to his rent-a-car … the registration plate was 214! These things happen in my life all the time, but I think Damian was quite amused and possibly a little intrigued. He gently asked me if I would be willing to be hypnotised, to see if there was anything in my memory that could aid in their search for evidence. He made it clear that anything that I remembered couldn't be used as evidence, but the hope was that it might lead to something more solid that could be used. He didn't specify, but I gathered that they were hoping I might remember seeing where my Mother's body was buried. Again, I struggled in my feelings of 'betraying' my father, but justified it in the sense that if he didn't do anything, then I wouldn't have anything in my memory to 'betray' him with! Synchronistically, my family's visit coincided with a Day of the Dead ceremony, honouring our ancestors who've passed over. So we gathered under the giant fig trees with photos or momentos of our loved ones and placed them at the base of the tree, among the gnarly roots; mine were photos of my beautiful Mother and I, and another one of Peter. Sharing these moments together was quite beautiful as I've mostly had to process grief on my own. The local choir sang songs, and we shared tears, poems, stories, humanity and hearts.

A Diary Entry

3rd of August 2013
New South Wales

Am wondering if I am 'supposed to' go to Sydney — as much as I want and need resolution to all this, I am also fearful of the repercussions this will have. Mostly on Sherry but also on the whole family dynamic crumbling. Would S and I even stay in touch? I wonder. I feel for her too. I realise it will be such a horrible shock for her. I hope Sherry will be okay. I don't actually think she'll believe the circumstantial evidence, unless they gain something more concrete. I wonder if it will bring us closer, or drive us further apart? I don't want to live a lie and that is one big, fat, fucking one!!

I am feeling the weight of the responsibility; what if what I remember sends my father to jail? Am I a piece of the missing puzzle, that could actually aid police in their search? I wouldn't want to betray my father, but honour my Mother and invite more peace into my own life, shed the light of truth onto the situation.

I did a short stint of being a nanny again, until the family moved back to Scotland, and I could redesign my life accordingly once more. I was really struggling with superficial small talk and couldn't relate much to people in such casual situations. I didn't know how to answer, 'How are you?' anymore; it seemed such a senseless, futile, superficial ritual. Most people don't actually want an authentic response and when they get one, you see them edging nervously toward the door, or avoiding you in the street. I was a mess. At this time, I felt most comfortable in quite intense situations, where I could drop down deep, holding space and being authentic. I had already done a doula (birth support) course while living in North America, so I decided this was the time to move forward with that. I did another local doula course to refresh my knowledge and inspirations as well as a volunteer hospice course through the Byron Community College, with the intention of gaining more experience and eventually combining that with my passion for conscious birthing and calling myself a soul doula. I wanted to offer my services to hold space, emotionally, spiritually and practically, for souls leaving their bodies and for souls being birthed onto the Earth.

During this time, there were moments where I felt good to have a purpose, something that felt real and hopeful and in the spirit of creating a kinder world. Then another part of me would take over and it was as if I couldn't access the part of me that cared. It made me feel so completely exhausted;

just feeding myself and washing a few dishes felt like a huge effort and accomplishment during those days. These times, I hid from the world.

On the 8th of January 2013 – K's birthday and the anniversary of my Mother going 'missing' – I dreamed of preparing for a huge storm or natural disaster. It was mostly dad, my sister and me. In the dream, I was told there was a third person involved in my Mother's murder. I also dreamed that my father was pressing himself against me inappropriately whilst holding a little girl captive and my sister and I were communicating with each other under water, like we did when we were little.

On the 9th of January, Damian (Loone) called to say they were setting a date for me to fly to Sydney, to see if I am susceptible to being hypnotised. I was impressed that when all other leads seemed to have run dry, Damian was willing to think outside the box and try an approach which isn't standard practice in his profession and I'm sure he copped a lot of flack for this; however, I think that just the fact something was being done ignited the Simms family's hopes a little again.

The year 2013 marked ten years since the last coronial inquest into my Mother's death. It was also the year NSW Police offered a $100,000 reward for any information on my Mother's case. I felt that if someone who previously knew something was only enticed to come forward because of a reward, then they didn't deserve it ... but I was also grateful and hoping that the police were doing all they could to help bring justice for my Mum.

A Series of Diary Entries

18th of March 2013
Sydney, New South Wales

Today I am in Sydney and meeting with Dr Banks (an ironically fitting name) to assess whether I can be hypnotised, to see if I have anything in my memory bank to help the case. It's strange being back in Sydney, surreal. I left my safe little bubble, to be picked up by police at the airport; I'm so out of my comfort zone but I must do it for my Mother, in the hope of justice and bringing the truth to light. I want my sister to know she loves us and didn't leave us of her own accord. I don't know what I will remember; I'm feeling scared and brave at the same time. Apparently, I'm a good subject and we've just made another appointment for next week, when we will do the actual hypnosis.

28th of March 2012
Full moon, New South Wales

I feel sick, nauseous.

I find myself making strange whimpering, puppy whines as though I'm sleeping. Crying for hours, lying with my mouth open, panting.

Write out the vile vomit, so life can taste sweet again.

Did I watch you strangle her? With your hands, or her blue belt?

My beloved Mother.

Whimpering noises again. Tears. Eyes rolling in my head.

Do I tell my family I'm working with police? I feel guilty but have done nothing wrong. I am not the one who has betrayed them, it is my father!

The night before my hypnosis, I had a dream where I clearly heard the phrase 'With his own bare hands'.

I didn't write about my hypnosis in my diary, I didn't want to relive it. I was picked up from the airport by a lovely female police lady and was so grateful for her sensitive approach. On the way to my appointment, we enjoyed a good, somewhat spiritual chat, which helped a little with my nerves. I was driven to the Chatswood Shopping Centre. We parked the car and as we walked through the bustling streets toward the office, the police lady gestured around. I didn't understand what she was referring to and looked at her quizzically. 'Look at the colours,' she said. Every single person within view in that moment was dressed in sharp black, grey or navy outfits. I stood there in non-tailored bright blues and greens – the only colour in sight – and found her observation bemusing. I was definitely feeling extremely out of place!

At Chatswood, we walked up the concrete stairs and into the elevator, which is symbolic for accessing different realms of consciousness. It's a fitting metaphor, except I should've been going waaayyy down 100 floors below the basement.

In the clinic, the doctor did what he could to put me at ease and it was certainly a similar feeling to when I went parachuting ... feeling compelled and overwhelmed, but holding my own (for that moment at least, until I fall apart later). Apparently, the doctor can tell by the movement of my eyeballs whether what I'm seeing are actual memories. He's trained to detect these movements.

It was quite fascinating. I was fully aware of adult Shanelle lying in the chair, but I could see, behind my closed eyes, what my four and a half-year-old self could see, and I could feel what she felt. I could consciously choose whether I spoke as if I was her, or through my adult interpretation of it. This is what came to me ...

I heard fighting; in my pyjamas and weary eyed, I'm now standing at the kitchen door, the bright lights causing me to squint and I feel confused and scared to see my father's hands are around my Mother's neck. I don't know if my screaming is just inside my head, or if it came out of my mouth.

Everything goes black and the next flash of memory I can access, I am in the back of the car, my sister is asleep beside me and my Mother is slumped in the front seat. I'm seeing her on the right, though I know logically she would be in the passenger side on the left. I'm trying to open my eyes but they're too heavy and I can't focus them. I don't know why, but my perspective shifts and I can see the scene before me as though from a bird's eye view. I find this curious, but the doctor prompts me to continue, reassuring me it's valid. I see the car, still in the driveway with the headlights pointing at the side of the dirt wall of the pool, the right-hand corner nearest to the house. My father is retrieving a shovel from the boot of the car, and I see him digging …

Black again …

Later on, a phone call on our old-fashioned looking phone … and nothing.

The doctor encouraged me to find more memories, where it had gone black, but I couldn't. Those images are clear, but in between it is like when a TV is trying to tune in to a channel. It is fuzzy and static, then momentarily there is a flash of an image which dissolves again before the pixels solidify; I keep trying to fine-tune …

Once again, I see the images that have long since baffled me: the front door, the teddy, the person taking me away from the door … and it registers that those images have always been clues, signalling to my conscious mind and trying to relay the truth. I saw glimpses of the next day at the baths, though nothing more than I've already shared in the earlier chapter. The anger I could feel when my four-year-old self was being told she was lying when she was not, was so tangible and alive though; the feeling stays with me, as does her confusion, her longing.

I couldn't access any more information from the catalogue of too traumatic recesses, unfortunately. I believe my father must've driven around trying to find somewhere before settling on that spot until he could move her the next day, once my sister and I were with family. After my appointment, I was quite disassociated as I wandered around The Rocks, where Damian was stationed. I remembered much happier, more oblivious times as I looked at Sydney Harbour and recalled the joy of catching the ferry with our Nanna and how excited she would get when there was a decent swell, rubbing her hands together and clapping. The familiar backdrop of the Opera House with the orchestra of city dock sounds, the salty air and seagulls squawking, all combined to concoct a potent mix of bittersweet emotion.

I had requested a copy of this regression – the notes and transcript from my hypnotist appointment – for me and also for my Mum's family. But, bizarrely, I was told that those recordings weren't able to be found, just like the files in my Mother's missing person's report.

The hypnotism raised more questions …

When I saw our old-fashioned looking phone, *who* did my father call in that moment?

When I was pulled away from the door by someone, *who* was it?

After my hypnosis, I dreamed of the names Bronwyn and Tanya. I dreamed of jail, and my whole family being separated in different compartments.

Is it in the highest good to confront my father? There was so much distance between us and I was experiencing such guilt for not telling my family I was being hypnotised. I don't really like him as a person. I don't feel that he enhances my life in any positive way, so I'm happy to 'bless and go'. I'd like to have clarity on whether my part in the police case has been actively played now the wheels of fate are in motion. Can I passively allow it to play out, or do I need to do more? I really don't have the capacity to confront my father … and really don't want to lose my sister.

I dreamed of my cousin and a huge whale, the Akashic record keeper. In a meditation, I hear the message: 'You don't need to understand something, to accept it.'

There's so much I don't understand. In my family in particular, the walls of illusion are built so thick and so high, they seem impenetrable. It's hard to know what's real. And harder still to speak out against popular opinion and say things as they really are. Am I being used as a scapegoat and having all sorts of shit projected onto me by my father? Why be jumping up and down, waving my arms in the air, if they're choosing to stay in their world of lies?

I couldn't play my father's games of make-believe happy families anymore. My father may have wanted me to be happy, easy-going 'Nelly' again, but she was a masquerade. I could no longer use my master puppetry skills to pull the strings. My father's love for me seemed so conditional, if it was even love at all.

In this semblance of the new, more real me, after my body of old programs and automatic responses and subconscious defence mechanisms had been completely blasted by the dynamite of life experience, I felt as though I couldn't be her anymore, even if I wanted to be. There were parts of her I missed, but I tried to find those qualities in a more genuine form from a deeper core of my being, many layers peeled and fallen away. My heart was always pure, but she was buried and it has taken her to be completely broken, stomped, grinded, twisted, tortured bloody raw to be opened to this new experience of life and to actively seek a more gentle and kind existence in this world, which is crucial to my rebirth and survival on this planet.

Every cell of my body and every atom of my being screams at me, a deafening, silent roar.

In the eighteen months since I'd been back in Australia after Peter died, I'd dreamed of him fairly regularly. In one dream, Peter was showing me photos of himself, and I asked him if there were any good ones. He said, 'Yeah, this one,' and showed me a photo of him grinning with his backpack. In another dream, Peter was still alive. I didn't want to wake up.

I was in a weekly group called 'Grief and Praise', which was beautifully supportive at this time in my life and some of the same people, including me, had also formed a choir called 'Bridgeweavers'. We were offering ourselves to sing and tone as women birthed, or for people who were dying. I felt really inspired by this group and our visions as they so closely aligned with the other passions I was pursuing. My doula career had just started to take off; I had teamed up with another doula friend and we were getting a good response.

Then for various reasons (nothing adverse), my services were not engaged for the first three births I had lined up.

I found myself with nothing laid out before me to move forward with. I was at another loose end in my life.

Around the same time, I had a very vivid dream with lots of detail about an adobe style healing centre and a community of people. Two days later (in real life), I saw the healing centre on a travel show! I didn't actually own a TV at the time, but had borrowed one from a friend because there was going to be something airing about my Mum and I wanted to watch it. Somebody had also given me a flyer for this same place in the Sacred Valley, in Peru. I couldn't deny I was being called to South America. I still felt a need to go to Brazil to see where Peter had died and where he was buried.

In June 2013, on a drive home in the Byron Shire, I saw a fox. The animal's eyes lit up in my headlights momentarily before its sly character and luscious fur disappeared into the night. I couldn't remember ever seeing a fox in the wild in Australia before.

As I said earlier, the fox was one of Peter's spirit animals.

I bought a flight to Peru on the 5th of August 2013, flying home from Brazil a couple of months later … and again, nothing booked in between …

CHAPTER NINE

Rites of Passage

It is somewhere around the 5th of August 2013; I've lost or gained a day in time, which is confusing to my brain. I am in the airport in Chile, on a stopover and on my way to Pisac, in the Sacred Valley, Peru, the place that came to me first in my dreams, then in a flyer and then in a travel show. I glance in my diary, at where I have transferred the directions to Peter's grave. His sister and I had some long, heartfelt conversations and she gave me these directions. From the city of Manaus in the Brazilian State of Amazonas, I had to take a flight or a two-day boat trip down the Rio Negro to the town of Barcelos. Peter was buried in the cemetery near the police station. He was the only Westerner there. While I sat in the airport awaiting my adjoining flight, slumped in a jet-lagged trance on the floor, a couple of sweet moments warmed my hurting heart. First there were two young boys with balloons; one of the balloons escaped and made its way to me and I passed it back to its rightful guardian. He stopped in complete intrigue and kept pointing at his hair and eyes and then mine; he couldn't stop staring until his mother led him away. Then there were these adorable mamitas – older, little ladies – who kept staring at me, then coming over and doing the sign of the cross over me and telling me I was beautiful ... this happened several times!

Once I finally arrived at the Sacred Valley, I had some amazing experiences there including a six-day hike out from Cuzco to Machu Picchu along the Salkantay Trail (an alternate route to the Inca Trail), including part of the Peruvian Andes. Machu Picchu is profoundly beautiful; its majesty and rich culture echoed whispers from ages past and affected me deeply.

Back in Cuzco, a small group of us visited an orphanage and I thought I might volunteer for some time. My limited Spanish was an obstacle, as was the fact that it's very difficult on the children to form a bond only to have it taken away. I know that heartache well. We went zip lining through deep valleys and one day a group of us hiked up into a cave and made a music video. My new Israeli friend and I planned to fly to Lima, then on to Iquitos, in the Peruvian Amazon. It is completely loco here, and I can't stop singing Guns N' Roses' 'Welcome To The Jungle' to myself! It's from Iquitos that I decide to set out on my own by boat, through to Manaus.

A Poem

11th of September 2013
Peruvian Amazon

White Owl Woman

Nourished by solitude
Deeply relishing the drinking of forest hues
Days of fighting and resisting invisible enemies
Silenced for now, by truce
I find again
The knowing of my inner sanctuary
And take refuge in her loving arms
La selva sings to me of love and connection
And untamed beauty,
As do I, to her
The rain joins for some tropical rhyme
Fireflies dance on the melodic waves of time
Flying increasingly closer to my eyes
Flirting with my senses
A chorus of crickets on soprano
The frogs on alto and bass
Were these the sounds that filled your ears
And accompanied your soul
On its journey
Home, Peter
My love?

A Dream

11th of September 2013
Peru

Of my father, Damian Loone and cups of milk spiked with Valium.

At two points on the three-day journey, I had to get off the boat to get my visa stamped. At the second border crossover, I stepped off the boat and as I hoisted my heavy backpack on, I felt a slight sting or bite on my hip.

A Diary Entry

Undated
Somewhere in Brazil

Long day on the boat so far; I'm the only gringo (white person) and nobody speaks English, nor do I speak Portuguese. I've spotted six river dolphins so far; their fins are a weird, stunted-looking shape. Imagine my concern when I woke up looking like the elephant man! My whole body is swollen, in particular my face and ears. My head and palms of my hands are sooo itchy! Must be toxemia from a suspected spider bite two days ago. The actual bite is extremely purple and red, very sore and swollen. It would be so terribly ironic to arrive to Peter's grave just to die there! And from a bite or sting, just like him. I have arrived to Manaus, Brazil, now and am waiting for the boat to Barcelos. Thankfully my face and ear swelling has gone down by about half and the bite has reduced in colour and size, from about a 50c piece to a 20c ... perhaps I'm not going to die after all ...?

168

When I arrived at Manaus, with a swollen face and my sturdy backpack, I made my way across the city to the dock where the boats left for Barcelos. There, I was told the boat wouldn't come for another two days. Oh, okay. South America definitely has its own, slow rhythm, and timetables seem to be more like guidelines. I managed to find a hostel, where my swelling eventually went down, and was back at the dock in two days, in time to watch the workers loading up the boat with boxes and boxes of soft drink and packets of junk, headed to the middle of the jungle. I really believe that these multinational companies need to take responsibility for the fact their products are being shipped to places that don't have the means or necessarily the education to recycle or 'dispose of thoughtfully'. Rubbish in Barcelos is burnt, or thrown and swept into the Rio Negro where you can see it, strewn and clinging to trees in remote villages and no doubt causing great harm and killing the life that inhabits the river.

I was shocked to see just how many boxes of 'necessities' were loaded onto the boat, and later I learned that these boats often overturn. I was grateful I wasn't aware of it at the time!

The boat stunk like diesel and was rough and loud as it chugged along. There was one main deck, with hammock hooks lined up in close proximity to each other. All of the locals hung their hammocks. I knew I needed one but didn't want to buy one just for a three-day boat trip and then have to carry it around. I laid out my things in the space my hammock would've otherwise occupied and when a man hung his hammock directly above my claimed space, I was pissed. It turned out to be a blessing in disguise as I found a spot at the front or bow of the boat, away from the masses of people slotted in like sardines. It was much quieter, apart from the chugging engine. I lay on top of my towel with some clothes as a blanket, though it was quite balmy in the tropics and the boat moved slow enough to not create a draft. I could see the stars and, as I have many times on my travels, prayed for the rain to hold off!

Leaving Manaus, I got to see the natural phenomenon – the Meeting of Waters – firsthand. For six kilometres, the dark black water of the Rio Negro runs side by side with the pale sandy-coloured white water of the Amazon River. The different coloured waters meet, but they don't mix, because of differences in the temperature, speed and sediment in the rivers. The result is a dual-toned river: one side dark, the other light. It's quite an amazing thing to see.

Brazilian pop music played on the deck during the day; the other passengers sang and seemed to know the songs and danced to the beat. Brazilians are definitely not shy and certainly know how to celebrate. For meals, one big pot was cooked up for everyone to share – you didn't get to pick from a menu. I was vegetarian at the time, but had resigned myself to eating whatever I was given. I was eating a bowl of stew when I realised that what I thought was penne pasta was actually intestine. I'm of the belief that if we're going to kill animals, we should be eating and utilising all the parts as much as possible, but it was too much of a stretch for me. The people sharing the table saw my face when I made the realisation and laughed their heads off. They happily finished the rest of the meal for me.

It was quite surreal being on the same boat, doing the same trip that Peter took to get to his final resting place. It felt fitting to be doing it that way. I asked him multiple times, why on earth he chose this place and how did he find it?! I saw lots of solo 'boto' (dolphins) on this trip – and lots of jungle.

The first thing I noticed about Eduardo was his bright orange hammock. We chatted on the front of the boat, toward the end of the journey. In broken English and Portuguese, he told me about his life, why he was heading to Barcelos for work, his family. I tried to explain why I was there, in my limited cave girl Spanish/Portuguese/English combination. I think he pretended to understand more than he did. I found it tiring and although it was nice to have my first 'real' conversation in almost a week, I kept trying to resort back to absorbing the surroundings in silence. I was wearing a soda can ring pull that Peter had put on my finger and jokingly proposed to me with. Eduardo noticed the ring on my wedding finger as we were talking and quickly leaped up. I hadn't realised he'd been flirting with me, but he must have been. I told him it was okay and we kept talking. He told me he wanted to introduce me to his family and teach me to Samba. A typical Brazilian!

When we departed the boat on arrival in Barcelos, I imagined I wouldn't see Eduardo again because he'd told me he was heading back to Manaus on the next boat, which was in three days. Three days later, as I heard the boat announce its departure with loud honking, I felt unexpectedly sad. I was surprised by this feeling as I hadn't been attracted to Eduardo, nor felt a strong connection. A few days later, I was surprised to run into Eduardo, who was still in Barcelos working with a couple of other guys putting up an awning outside a shop. We said hello, he introduced me to his friends, and I told him where I was staying. After work, every day he'd show up at my hostel cleanly showered and dressed, wanting to take me out for a kebab. His persistence was simultaneously annoying and endearing. Once Eduardo accompanied me to the cemetery, where he saw a photo of Peter and me, and he got all dramatic, turned to me and said, 'You never look at me like that.'

I wasn't in love with Eduardo, and I had never pretended to be; he felt like an annoying but kind of loveable puppy who wouldn't leave me alone. I liked him in a confusing kind of way and enjoyed his company – and I was grateful to have a friend and ally in Barcelos; he was very attentive and we laughed together a lot at first.

A Dream

23rd of October 2013
Barcelos, Brazil

I've lied about being able to surf — or have been
misunderstood. I'm out in HUGE waves and am very scared.
There are three of us. My dad is with me. Finally, we
get to the edge where it's calm and hang on to the edge.
I think of the expression, 'In way over my head.'

I found Peter's grave on the very first night I got to Barcelos. I walked straight to it, like I knew where it was, which is pretty amazing given how many graves are here and that it was dark. I went back to the cemetery almost every day and was fortunate to still be there to pay my respects on their Day of the Dead celebrations in early November.

When I first got to town, the river was high so I couldn't travel to the exact spot where Peter had died. It took some time and research to eventually get to the area. There were only two or three people who spoke English in the village. One of them was the German doctor who had done Peter's autopsy with his dad and who told me roughly how to get to where he was found, but she was busy so I didn't want to ask too much of her. I dreamed of a black feather, which turned into an owl feather, I found a ring … and I was handed a black baby. Momentarily forgetting my dream, the next day I left an owl feather at Peter's grave, along with the 'ring' he'd given me and then found a black feather near where he died.

I was sitting off the side of the dirt road, at the closest accessible spot to where Peter had died, alongside a small bridge. I was crying and singing when a guy on a motor scooter pulled up and indicated he knew where it was that Peter had died. He said he would come by my hostel, which he did, and the Dutch hostel owner (the only other English speaker that I met) translated that he would take me to the spot where Peter had died, once the waters had receded.

That day came, which coincided with their Day of the Dead ... a new moon and solar eclipse, the 2nd of November. The hostel owner, Eduardo and one of his friends came too. I took my drum and a harpy eagle feather I'd been given. Once at the spot, I told the group of men to go so I could be on my own. I sat, cried, drummed, prayed and meditated, then cried some more. I found a vine that had been twisted into a circle (probably for fishing) and made a dreamcatcher out of it with some hemp string I had along with the magnificent feather. I hung it from one of the trees where Peter's hammock had been. I took a photo with my shitty old Nokia phone of the exact spot Peter had left his body, and the sun formed a perfect rainbow portal with the dreamcatcher faintly visible inside it. It was a special moment.

The evening came. *Dia dos Mortos*. I lit a candle for Peter, and for his mum, dad, sister and nephew. The whole village seemed to be there and the entire cemetery was lit up with candles, prayers and songs. It felt beautiful to be a part of that.

When I wasn't processing Peter's death or trying to find out more information about his final days, I was spending time with Eduardo and the meeting of the lapping waters was like the meeting of our two worlds. I didn't get attached to Eduardo as I doubted his sincerity until the first time I tried to leave and he cried. I found that really confusing, because either I'd been projecting all of my trust issues onto him, or he deserved an Academy Award! Or maybe a bit of both?

Saturday nights there was some form of music and entertainment in the village, where people would drink and dance. On Eduardo's only full day off, Sunday, we used to take a tinny over to an island (once the waters had receded enough) where we swam and had picnics. I went over on a weekday and picked up as many garbage bags full of rubbish that we could fit in the tinny. I would get so disgusted by all the rubbish, but the people simply don't know the damage they are doing, nor are there better options in place. His friends would invite me over for hot meals on his lunch breaks and we'd hang out together after he finished work. I did some artwork for a local business and went fishing a few times. The days were oppressingly hot (we had a week of 50 degrees!), some days we were just lolling around in front of the fan until the relief from the heat made it possible to move! The village would come alive when the sun went down and there would be so many people out for a walk at dusk. No air-conditioning, by the way, just fans!

I had been dreaming of Peter, when my alarm went off for my 7 am breakfast date one morning. The dream was set at his house and the police were dealing with his sister and his bank accounts. So secretive Peter was … always so many unknowns with him. I asked the police about his credit card, not interested in his money but in where he'd been. He had a canoe with a paddle, and the police showed me how to use it. I was in Peter's car, inside a library, the music was loud and I turned it down, then we hit a bump and it went loud again. 'Is Peter trying to tell me something through my dreams?' I wondered. I could feel my grief fading a little being there, and though it still came in waves, the waves slowly became further apart and less intense.

Another new moon had come and gone, and I was waiting to bleed but it didn't come … My moon cycle was rarely late, but I figured it was probably from the stress of travelling, or maybe I had a parasite. I ended up taking a pregnancy test and it came back negative. I remember feeling relieved, but also a little disappointed. I've asked Peter that if there's a reason I'm still here, please let it be known; I've been trying to leave for a month now!

On the 6th of November, Eduardo returned home to Manaus as his work in Barcelos was finished. I was ready to leave as well; Barcelos had become like the movie *Groundhog Day* for me. When I first arrived, I found it a novelty that everyone would stare at me. I towered over everybody there by at least a head, I was the only person with blue eyes in the whole village, but after seven weeks of being there, I was over it. I tried at least three times to leave but couldn't do so. The first time, the computer froze while I was trying to book a seat on the boat back to Manaus. The second time, when it was cloudy, the internet wouldn't work. I went to the 'office' a few times and nobody was home. At the 'port' (a plank of thick wood), I was told the boat was full. I tried to fly out, but the plane didn't come that day, then there wasn't a spare seat on the next one … So I had to let go of the return flight back to Australia that I had pre-booked (I couldn't even contact the airline to change the date). For some reason, the universe wanted me to stay in Barcelos for a little longer; maybe there was a reason for it?

At some point while I was there, a young man and his mother approached me at the smoothie shop I frequented. I was madly looking up words in the pocket-sized Portuguese/English dictionary I had. He claimed that Peter's cause of death was incorrect and that he was the first to find Peter dead, before the police got to him. He told me it wasn't an accident. He said it was murder. He told me he had photos if I wanted to see them.

I struggled to decide, but concluded I didn't want to see the photos. My last memory was of him smiling, as he walked out his front door, then of him texting me to say he'd missed his bus and seen a fox. I didn't want my last memory of Peter to be of a photo of him, dead. I also didn't know if it was safe to go and meet a stranger on a boat in the middle of the Amazon, where I didn't know anyone.

There were questions and a certain mystery surrounding Peter's death, and as much as I wanted answers, I felt vulnerable chasing them. During my time in the town, I learned that the German doctor who'd done the autopsy on Peter was married to a man who did medicine ceremonies. I can imagine Peter being involved in such a ceremony. He was on a healing journey, hoping to get help for his mental health issues. I'd been told by someone in the village that the medicine man was the last person to be seen with a couple of backpackers who went missing in the area. He had also been seen with Peter. I don't know if the person who told me this information was insinuating that the medicine man had something to do with Peter's death. I never got the chance to meet the medicine man, and I was also scared to. I told Peter that if I was there to reveal answers and truths, that I needed someone I could trust, who could translate for me.

In the six or seven weeks I ended up being in Barcelos, I didn't find my answers. I may never know the details of what happened, and I've had to make my peace with that, just as I've tried to do that with the unknowns surrounding my Mother's death.

I met up with Eduardo one last time in Manaus before my flight to Bahia in the northeast of Brazil, where I was going to explore more of the country. We spent a few lovely hours together where he took me swimming and introduced me to some of his family members and we said our goodbyes, and once again I thought I would never see Eduardo again.

I had hired a car in the city of Salvador, Brazil, and was on a two-week road trip, staying in a *pousada* (hostel) near Chapada Diamantina National Park, thoroughly enjoying some time to myself again. My cosy room had a window with the view of a hammock strung up between two posts on the veranda. It was the 26th of November; my moontime still hadn't come, so I did another pregnancy test. Deep breath. It was positive, I was pregnant. 'Oh fuck, my whole life is about to change,' I thought to myself. I took a photo of the hammock because I knew I'd want to document this pertinent moment.

A Diary Entry

4th of December 2013
Salvadore, Brazil

I returned the [hire] car yesterday. What a trip, only two weeks but feels like a lifetime. I left believing I wasn't pregnant and returned knowing I am. Yesterday I kept seeing my lucky numbers and this morning have woken to two owls on the roof, only a few metres away. They were preening each other and appeared to be cuddling; one would rest its head on the other. I noticed when I was in between dreaming and waking states, I referred to the baby as 'she'... interesting, noted.

I meditate on the beach, where I connect with the spirit of the baby and show her what I had hoped and held out for so long ... for a conscious conception, with a beautiful man and of us being deeply in love. I stated though, that if it was 'in the highest good', then she was welcome to stay. I believe I could feel her response to me, not hear it in words, but feel what she was saying ... she agreed that my vision was lovely, but that she had things to do and was coming in.

Okay then, here we go ...

I always knew I wanted to be a mother someday and felt impatient for the experience, though I hadn't yet met a man I wanted to spend my whole life with. During a women's new moon circle, in a yurt and by candlelight, we were invited to write a letter to our future daughters, of what we would wish them to know for their first moon cycle. It's knowledge I would've loved to have gotten from my own Mother, so my first period wasn't as lonely and unsupported as it was. The intention is to reclaim sacred rites of passage in our lacking (white) culture. The letter reads ...

With candles lit, flowers and natural beauty surrounding you, as well as mothers, aunties, grandmothers, sisters and daughters ...

The shedding of your uterus is often simultaneously released with tears and they are welcome.

The internal ebb and flow of our moon-cycle is conducted by the silvery magic of our maestress moon.

180

We, as receptive vessels, gather, hold and transmute energy
in our sacred wombs. All women are embodiments of Mother
Earth, shedding what no longer serves us like the shedding of an
outworn skin.

Let's embrace our seasonal bodies and celebrate with song,
stories, laughter and tears.

Allow yourself to feel held and nourished by this circle of women
and enchanted by the feminine mystery you are now initiated into.

Adorned in rose petals, anointed in Earth balms and knowing to
the core of your being — your sacred Earth body is beautiful.

Of course, when I wrote the letter, I didn't know if I would
have a daughter in the future. Or maybe on some level I
did …?

My beautiful Mum when she was two.

Uncle Greg's christening – with Pa, Nanna Simms,
Uncle Phil, Auntie Pat and my Mum on far right.

Mum swimming at the Bogey Hole.
She was definitely a water baby.

My Mother and father – happy days.
I love my Mother's joy as she places the
garter on my father's leg.

My father, Mother, Nanna and Pa at my Mum's nursing graduation.

This photo was taken at Uncle Greg and Auntie Merilyn's wedding, with Mum and dad, Uncle Phil and his wife, Lynda, and Auntie Pat. My Mum is about four-weeks pregnant. I wonder if she knew?

After trying for children for many years, Mum finally held me in her arms. Two years later, my sister was born. I am told my Mother loved her girls more than anything and would never have left us.

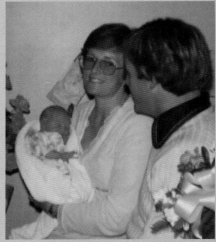

This was the last known photo of my Mother ever taken. She is next to my father at the piano during the Christmas party for the childcare centre she worked at.

Singing 'Happy Birthday' in Slovenian; kissing the Sphinx in Egypt; planting trees in Mexico.

The Kombi called Kiala; my Colorado kiddies and me at a parade; Taz and Jezebel the hiking cat; hang-gliding in Turkey; and a village in Mexico where we were doing environmental education.

Me in our infinity garden in Glastonbury, paying respect to my Mother. Meditating by a
waterhole in Airlie Beach.

Doodles from my journals: Spain, Greece, Portugal, Italy and Holland. Butterflies represent my Mum.

Peter and me in Glastonbury; journalling by the river in Peru; the portal of Peter in Brazil.

I wish my Mum could be here with us, she would have been a loving and wonderful Grandmother.
Kialah the water baby, swimming year round like her Nanna Lyn.

In Aotearoa (New Zealand).

Laying flowers with Auntie Pat at a walk organised
at Long Reef to honour my Mum.

Uncle Greg and Auntie Merilyn
visiting me and Kialah on the
Sunshine Coast.

CHAPTER TEN

Birthing a Mother

I don't know if it's poetic or macabre that I conceived my daughter within a kilometre of where my big love Peter died in the Amazon.

I returned back to Northern New South Wales from Brazil at the end of 2013 and found myself housesitting while I looked for a home.

I was only about two months pregnant when I returned. When I told my sister my news, her response was hilarious and completely non-judgemental. 'Thank God!' she exclaimed. 'We're not getting any younger!'

My father and stepmother had very generously offered me $70,000 for a deposit on a house loan/mortgage. It was an amazing offer and I understand that their intentions were good, but it came with the condition that I would be working full time. So when I told my father I was going to have a baby, although he was 'happy' for me, they subsequently withdrew their monetary offer.

I am afraid of being judged for the fact I haven't got a career. I would love to have the mental health capacity to hold down a full-time job again and I hope that one day I will. I never imagined the toll this whole situation would take on me or how taxing it's been on every level. I am fully aware I've accrued a debt to society; I'm incredibly grateful for the supports in place that have allowed me to raise my child and maintain a decent quality of life while my mental health has, understandably, taken a dive. I know I will repay this debt wholeheartedly.

I had found a studio to move into in Northern New South Wales, which became available in two weeks, so I headed to the Sunshine Coast in Queensland to visit my dear friend there, who was also pregnant and due *on the same day*, the 13th of July. It was a new moon, and I received a text telling me that my future landlords had changed their minds about renting out the house down south. I was upset but could also feel the wheels of fate in motion, so surrendered to that. My friend and I were driving in an intentional community to pick up a drum for our women's new moon circle that night. As we passed a little cottage we both felt something and turned to each other and said, 'Did you feel that?!' The owner of the cottage happened to be at the river for the gathering and confirmed the cottage was indeed for rent. As we shared, in our circle, a common theme I noticed was that a majority of the women there had moved to this particular community to give birth. Sometimes life works in mysterious ways. So, my growing belly (womb) and I relocated.

I always thought I would be a glowing Earth Mother, but instead I was a nauseous, bloated and irritable one; just keeping it real! Being pregnant was difficult; relocating and starting all over again in a place where I only knew a couple of people and while in such a vulnerable situation was painful. Not finding my midwife until about a week before I was due was testing to say the least! I will always love and appreciate the people in our lives at this time, who were there in the capacity they were able to be.

I had emailed Eduardo while still in Brazil and told him I was pregnant with his baby, and he pleaded for me to stay. I wanted to return to Australia to raise my child. We stayed in touch over email and Facebook, but Eduardo wasn't able to offer support or be involved, and I didn't expect him to.

During this time, I deeply felt the massive fucking black, gaping hole where a Mother should be. Oh how I longed for my Mother, more than ever in my adult life. It was cruel that I'd been robbed of having her there to celebrate, support me, give advice, answer my questions, cook me meals and help with the baby. Obviously, going through pregnancy and birth without a partner, and without a Mother, was yet another dagger to my heart. I know that living in that kind of heightened state and chronic stress takes a massive toll on one's life, health and heart.

A Dream

*My father and one other are preparing to be expelled
out of jets; it's understood they will die. We're looking
at a map to choose the location of where they will be
expelled. It seems it's up to me to press the button.*

On the 11th of April 2014, my sister Sherry got married. She didn't invite me to be in the bridal party, with the excuse that she knew I wouldn't want to wear heels or make-up, but she did honour our bond by having me read a passage from the Bible at their ceremony. The whole family, excluding my sister, were getting dressed at my father and stepmother's house where we were all staying for the weekend. K and my other siblings occupied the guest rooms at the house, while pregnant me was allocated the couch. When it came time to get ready, the bathrooms were in use, leaving me with no room to get dressed, so I got changed in the garage. It wasn't a big deal, but again, it was another subtle reminder of how my family treated me as inferior. We all piled into my father's van to drive to the wedding and when we pulled up to drop something off to my sister, we were instructed to stay in the car. I wish I'd insisted on seeing my sister as she prepared for her wedding. I had the garter from my Mother and father's wedding to give to her and *really* wanted to give her a massive hug, as her sister and in place of our Mother. I didn't know if it would upset her too much to receive the garter, as she was never very open to talking about our Mother with me, or if she would even want to see me. Internally, I anxiously debated what to do. I hesitated too long and missed my opportunity. I tried really hard, in my head and in my heart, to make this occasion all about my sister, but it was painful for me to be around my father. I also discovered on this day that as well as the family members I already knew weren't talking to me, now one of my father's older brothers and his wife weren't talking to me either ... I really should've cut ties with this family long before I did, but I hung in there for my sister.

At the reception, my sister and father took to the dance floor for the dad/daughter dance and were soon joined by my uncle and one of his daughters. My sister gestured for me to join her; oh, how in a completely different world that would've been a beautiful moment to share with her – and for her sake I really wanted to. It took all of my remaining sanity not to turn into a screaming banshee and wail down the whole place at the thought of having to dance with my father and fake being a happy family. I instead patted my belly and feigned pregnancy exhaustion.

I wished so much that our beautiful Mother was there in body to see her beloved daughter get married, though I believe she was there in spirit and I was so grateful to my sister's new husband who acknowledged that in his speech.

For many nights after my sister's wedding, I dreamed of various members of my family. In one dream, a family member came over and I hid. In another, I was in the house and they came home; I got scared and quickly left. Then there was a dream where my father and two of my uncles were sitting in a hot tub. I was stepping over their towels and angry my father had never told me about the hot tub, nor invited me to use it. Twice I dreamed my father was diving into deep water.

⟞⟨⟩

After intensely labouring all afternoon and all night, I gave birth to my baby girl on the morning of the 21st of July 2014. Once I met her and made sure the name fit, I named her Kialah, after the name that came to me while I was driving my green kombi van on a freeway in Colorado, though I added an 'h' to the original spelling to soften it a little. Her middle name is Elyn, a combination of Helena (Nanna) and Lyn (my Mum).

It was all extremely daunting and having to navigate becoming a mother all on my own was massively overwhelming. I did my best, but a loving Mother would've made a world of difference.

When Kialah was about a week old, my father, stepmother, two of my sisters and their husbands came to meet her. My sister had cooked me up lots of meals, which was the best gift;

they were all generous with their gifts and I was so grateful! On the surface it was a loving family visit. I genuinely wish it was just that.

I felt weird introducing my baby to my family, especially my father. I love them, but I felt quite estranged from them by this point. Still, I went through the motions even though the grief made me want to wail.

It should have been such a beautiful moment, but there was an underlying tension. My sisters refused to use my compost toilet, preferring to wait until they went into town thirty minutes away to use the public toilet. The fact they thought public toilets would be cleaner was so offensive to me. I tried to explain that compost toilets when working efficiently don't smell, that you can't see anything and that the ones at national parks aren't set up properly, giving compost loos a bad reputation. My family and I have so little in common!

Uncle Greg and Auntie Merilyn also visited us. Seeing them hold my daughter was less bittersweet, and more sweet. They went to a lot of effort and brought some beautiful baby gifts. My auntie is very good at craft and she had made me and Kialah handmade quilts and gone to a lot of care to put my favourite colours in mine. It was so special. I've missed out on a lot of things not having a Mum, so my auntie's love and effort meant the world to me.

Once I became a mother, things shifted internally for me regarding my own Mother/father wounds. What had been taken away from me now extended to my child, and as my somewhat fierce mama bear instincts activated, shit became even more real for me as it wasn't just me being affected in the dynamic with my father anymore.

I still had the internal battle of both loving and despising my father; seeing him hold my daughter perpetuated that confusion and made me feel that he hadn't earned the right to enjoy being her grandfather. He lit up when he saw her, and was a doting and mostly attentive grandfather. It broke my heart that my daughter and I couldn't just have that authentically. She deserved to have a grandpa in her life, just like she deserved to have a grandmother. But because of my father's actions, she was robbed of both.

I wanted Kialah to have people who love her in her life; I didn't want it to just be me. S was lovely and made a bit of a fuss, though the comparison to how she would come to dote on and behave toward her 'real' grandchildren was glaringly obvious, it just made me want to scream and hit my father that it wasn't my daughter's grandmother holding and loving her.

I knew I would never leave my daughter alone with my father. As my sisters went on to have children, I prayed but kept quiet that they too would be safe from harm – even indirect harm like subtle emotional abuse, which my sisters appeared blind to. I knew it was only a matter of time before I would have to have an extremely awkward moment and explanation of why my daughter wouldn't be left in my father's care.

The decision as to when I would withdraw from the family weighed on my conscience. I didn't want my daughter to feel overly bonded with my father and then take that away from her. And I didn't want to lose the rest of my family when I cut ties with my father. Though, had I known my sister would completely cut us off and that Kialah would lose her cousins as well … would I have hung in there as long as I did? Hard to say.

I didn't have much time to ponder those big questions in the thick of new motherhood. Those first weeks are very overwhelming until you find your mama rhythm, but it does kick in. The brain adapts to not sleeping much and you find ways of juggling everything, how to get things done with a baby strapped to you. Exhaustion and frustration go hand in hand with beauty and wonder.

At the cottage where we lived, there were a few resident pythons, which I usually love, until one of our neighbours found her two-year-old with a python wrapped around her legs, while she played on their veranda. It was so lucky it didn't make it to her neck; it took three grown men to pry it off her! I didn't leave my baby alone anyway, but now she accompanied me every moment and I did thorough checks under the bed before placing her on it.

A Diary Entry

23rd of December 2015
Sunshine Coast, Queensland

Sometimes we have to fall apart.

Like a house, sometimes we renovate sections at a time and other times it becomes apparent that it's necessary the whole building be demolished, ground zero and below. As we reassemble who we are, sometimes we can resurrect and salvage some of the old parts and others we recognise as parts of an old paradigm that no longer applies, other people's projections and ideas of who we should be and parts we've played out in order to fit those and be loved and accepted by others.

During this process of my reconstruction/rebirth I've learned a lot about myself. I see so many of the effective defence mechanisms and complications I've created as well as their reasons for existing. Haha, this doesn't mean they've ceased to exist, I just recognise them and do my best to keep things simpler, to avoid becoming overcrowded in unnecessary intricacies and yet I've also become more acutely aware of everything.

I see, feel and hear everything amplified as well as the unspoken, what's written between the lines, in the tilt of a head or sigh, tensing in the body or spoken with intention and undertones.

I feel all of the emotions in a room and can't always identify or separate them from my own, until I have space to process them away from everybody.

Becoming acutely aware of the world around me made it harder to ignore the gaping wound my father had inflicted upon me. I struggled to act 'normal', to keep up appearances, to remain calm when all I wanted to do was scream. I didn't quite feel ready to confront my father. I didn't want the responsibility, the burden of rocking the boat. It seemed there was always a birthday, engagement, wedding, anniversary, pregnancy, birth, and I didn't want to bring doom to these occasions. I didn't feel it was fair that I would be ostracised for what my father had done, as I assumed the rest of the family wouldn't believe me. I also didn't know if my child and I would be safe. I didn't know how my father and the rest of the family would react toward me. I didn't know if I could hold myself in the aftermath and still be a good mother. So, I wrote. I wrote my feelings and dreams in my diary as I've always done, and I also wrote a number of letters to people as a conflict resolution strategy. Most letters I never sent or gave to the person. I penned multiple letters to my father, as a way of releasing the toxic emotions from my being, but also rehearsing for the moment, should it arrive, that felt right to actually give them to him.

An Unsent Letter

October 2016
Sunshine Coast Hinterland, Queensland

To my father,

You have brought me into this world and I am made up of you and my Mother combined. I have loved you for thirty-nine years. Except that now I love and despise you, for now I know the truth of what you've done and of the utter selfishness you've acted upon. I can't go on pretending. I choose to live an authentic life. One where upon mutual agreement, people take responsibility for their actions and the way in which they affect others.

I'm know you think I'm just a lazy hippie (as you've implied it many times), but I don't need you to devalue me. I choose to respect myself and to know my worth. I know who I am and I love her. I have been working on myself for many years. I know internal workings don't count in your eyes, but I have been undoing all of the damage caused by you and by others during my childhood. A lot of self honesty has been necessary. I know the levels of integrity I hold and the compassion and empathy I'm capable of.

Do you understand how much it's fucked me up? Feeling both love and hate for you simultaneously and trying to reconcile both parts. To comprehend that the father who I once dearly loved, respected, adored and looked up to, was capable of things I can't comprehend.

That you aren't the person you pretended to be? To witness you in honesty, would be much easier to forgive, but how do you admit such an awful truth to yourself? It makes sense to me that you would have to believe your own illusion, in order to function and survive, but the cracks have shown themselves over the years.

Each time I see you I'm constantly confronting myself with your fucked up game of pretence and I can't keep fucking myself up like that anymore.

I do still love you and I always will, but you have broken my heart, shattered and grinded and violently ripped it into smithereens. Painful, bloody, pounding, raging, despairing, hopeless, utterly dismayed, betrayed beyond belief, beaten to a pulp and left dangling, crucified to die an excruciating death.

Even these words barely come close to describing the intensity of the sensations I've been processing, trying to digest and assimilate into ordinary reality. My defence mechanisms that have served me so well no longer exist. I've carried your burdens for too long, I choose to give you back your burdens, father. These were your choices, not mine. My foundations have long since crumbled and it breaks my heart to potentially walk away from the only family I've known but it's all based on lies and I choose to walk free.

It wasn't just my father that I had unresolved issues with. Becoming a mother and learning about children's developmental needs made me realise how traumatic the years after my Mother disappeared were. My sister and I were children who needed nurturing, tenderness and care and we didn't get these things. Looking at my own little girl, it's impossible to imagine her being treated as I was.

I understand J was groomed by my father. I understand that initially, by law, she was just a child. And I understand that she was escaping a shitty home life of her own. However, I left home at seventeen and also worked as a babysitter from when I was thirteen years old. I'm grateful that in the twenty or so families I've babysat and nannied for, never once did any of those dads ever make any passes at me. No matter what, I would never have allowed it regardless of what promises they might have made! Although J was a child, surely she still would have known that having sex with a married man was not okay, especially in my Mother's house, with her there and my Mother being slipped Valium, as she claims. I can't imagine being brainwashed to such an extent that you would think that was okay on any level. I still struggle to accept what happened.

I blame my father and our patriarchal society, but J made her own regrettable choices in the situation too. I do wish J had gone to live with her father or one of her older sisters; I'm not saying that there would have been a different outcome but maybe there might have been.

Again, I wrote to process my hurt. Here are parts of my unsent letter to her:

A Letter to J

8th of January 2017
Sunshine Coast, Queensland

To J,

It is the anniversary of my Mother's 'disappearance' and ironically your daughter's birthday, and I'm unable to sleep ...

I have accessed deeper layers of anger, rage, injustice and so I write to try to neutralise the toxic poison that I feel inside. I want you to know that after all of these years I'm still affected, as is my mothering and general character ...

It is only as an adult that I realised how fucked up it all was ...

We were good and kind children and didn't deserve how we were treated. You were a poor substitute for a mother.

I know you didn't have a good upbringing and that you were too young to become an instant mother when you were groomed by my father. I understand that in the eyes of the law, you were still a child, and certainly my father is very charming, manipulative and convincing, but even at sixteen, seventeen ... and then eighteen, you must've known the choices you were making were really shitty toward my Mother and her children?!

I'm not sure if these words have portrayed how much my sister and I missed out on a normal, happy childhood because of your actions ... I hope you can be both honest and compassionate with yourself. I don't wish you any harm.

Shanelle

When Kialah was three and a half years old, we set out to move to Aotearoa (New Zealand). I wanted to create a good life for us and I felt a deep connection to those lands, but I also wanted to put some distance between my father and us. I had intended on cutting ties from there, but I didn't end up selling my car and my father let me park it in the street outside their house, as well as keeping my few remaining boxes of belongings for me, so that plan took a different twist. We loved it in Aotearoa and had an amazing adventure, but unfortunately, I needed a home, kindy and a job to line up before my savings ran out. As they dwindled, we returned to Australia and decided to give living in Hervey Bay a try, as the cost of living was less than the Sunshine Coast where we'd been living previously, and I really wanted to be closer to the ocean but without the over-population of the Sunshine Coast.

My wish came true. We moved to a cute little beach cottage only a block away from the sea. What I loved most was that when the whales migrate along the coastline, they come in very close as they love the warm, sheltered waters of the bay. We actually had a TV for the year we lived in the cottage and after having not really watched TV for twenty years, I went through a phase where I would watch interviews with murderers. They say the eyes are the windows to the soul. I found myself studying the eyes of these people for clues to detect some giveaway sign that they are capable of such a drastic action, void of empathy, in order to attempt to understand my father and come to terms with how he was capable of doing such a thing. I noticed some eyes were vacant, whilst others were intense and predator-like.

When someone you love is capable of murder, it's so difficult to comprehend. It is 'crazy making', one psych I saw for a while would say, and I found this so validating. My wavering mental health was circumstantial and perhaps amplified by my exquisite sensitivity, or perhaps the reason for it.

In Hervey Bay, Kialah went to kindy two days a week while I returned to university to study human services. I had wanted to do counselling, but the campus I was enrolled in didn't offer that course. It was while Kialah was in care for the first time that her 'quirks' became more obvious. She was becoming overstimulated and doing sensory things like eating everything (paint, Blu Tack, etc), which by her age she should've been growing out of. Her meltdowns became more frequent and then at kindy she started ripping out her hair and eating it. I came to understand these behaviours as autistic traits, though it took three years to arrive at that diagnosis and that was another extremely stressful journey.

While all this was happening, I got a call. My Mum's family reached out to tell me about a podcast. I didn't actually know what a podcast was (I didn't have Wi-Fi or the time for such things), but they explained that a journalist named Hedley Thomas was producing a series about my

Mum's disappearance. At first, I was a bit taken aback but once it sunk in, I felt hopeful. I was grateful something was happening as there had been a long lull of inactivity on the justice front and I was worried my Mum's family had largely, if not entirely, given up hope of the truth coming to light. With the coronial inquests and police investigations, they'd been on a traumatic roller-coaster of promise, only to have their hopes dashed time and time again.

Greg, Pat and Merilyn were involved in the podcast, and when they asked me, I also agreed to take part in an interview as it felt right to honour my Mum. I wanted to show respect to my Mum, but I also felt guilty, as though I was betraying my father and immediate family. I was clear that I was not participating to accuse or avenge my father at all, but solely to honour my Mum and pierce the deafening silence regarding her 'disappearance'.

None of us could have expected what happened next. I was entirely naive about the vast implications the podcast would have. I thought it might help to give us some answers, but it ended up stirring up far, far more than that ...

CHAPTER ELEVEN

Last Father's Day

The Teacher's Pet podcast premiered in May 2018. The title *The Teacher's Pet* came from The Police song 'Don't Stand So Close to Me', about a teacher having an affair with his student. The story behind the podcast had it all – sex, lies, murder and intrigue – except it wasn't just an entertaining story to me. It was my life. I was told the podcast was to find answers about my Mum so when I first heard the title, I told Hedley I felt it put the focus on my father and J, not on my Mother, but they decided it was a good fit.

When Hedley asked me if I was open to speaking with him, I did so on the provision that I wouldn't speak about my father or his possible guilt. I only wanted to honour my Mother. When Hedley came to interview me, my Auntie Pat came and spent some time with Kialah; this was really special to me and Kialah.

Each week, as *The Teacher's Pet* podcast was released, my Mum's family and I hung on every word. We were longing for a piece of evidence that would come and bring us answers and much needed closure.

We weren't the only ones; hundreds of thousands of people tuned into the episodes along with us. Within the first six months, the podcast was downloaded 28 million times. The podcast went to number one on the charts. It won a Gold Walkley Award for investigative journalism. Photos of my Mother, father, J, my sister and me appeared in newspapers, magazines and online. My last name became infamous. It was strange and surreal being recognised by strangers a handful of times. Most of my friends (like me) don't read or watch mainstream news, so most of the people closest to me were largely oblivious to it all, unless I shared it with them. And to be honest, it was difficult sharing my Mum with the world when I didn't feel I'd had enough of her myself. There were photos being posted I'd never seen and I wished people would think to send them to me privately, rather than my stumbling upon them on social media. I was so depleted from expressing how much I had struggled over the years, it would be a lovely day when this stress was behind me and I could hold the love for my Mother in a different place, in a softer and more private space once again.

Although I was getting excellent grades at university where I was still studying human services, the emotional demands of the grief and trauma of my father murdering my Mother, still maintaining a connection with him, single mothering and the additional stress of the podcast were causing more undeniable cracks in my mental health. During an assessed presentation at uni, I choked back tears and almost broke down crying!

It was such a weird and heavy time. Understandably, the podcast stirred up a lot of emotions in me: sadness, hurt, betrayal and anger. I had so much rage – not just at my father, but also at the authorities and systems that had failed my Mother so miserably. My feelings toward my father continued to exist in a headlocked internal polarity battle.

It was so strange witnessing something that is such a part of my inner world, playing out for the masses to witness. So many different opinions and judgements of my father and my Mother, happening despite and in absence of me ...

It was hard hearing these stories and opinions alongside 28 million other people. The foundations of my whole life had long since crumbled and I was sorting through the ruins, trying to differentiate between truth and lies ... Did my father really love my Mother in the beginning, or was he just 'love bombing' her? At what point did their relationship sour? It was so confronting hearing again about the evidence I'd already read in police briefs, about the bruises and myriad ways my father dishonoured my Mother.

In the podcast episode titled 'Bruises', a dressmaker in the Strand Arcade in Sydney's CBD remembers seeing bruises on my Mother's body when she was taking her measurements for a dress. There were finger-shaped bruises on my Mum's arms and a huge ugly bruise on her thigh. It looked like she'd been kicked. The dressmaker was shocked and asked my Mum what had happened. 'Oh, well, it's a long story,' my Mum is said to have replied. 'I'm married to a very violent man.'

'Why don't you leave him? Why not just get away to be free of the violence and pain?' the dressmaker asked.

'Well, it would be difficult. I wouldn't know where to go,' Mum explained.

The recollection supported statements made by my Mother's friends that she would never leave us. I'm grateful to her friends who persisted to achieve justice, knowing that something didn't quite add up and that she would never abandon her children, knowing how much she loved us.

I was reminded of something my Mother relayed to her work colleague and friend – that on the last day my Mother was seen, as she and my father were on their way to a marriage counselling session, he grabbed her by the throat and threatened her. 'I'm only doing this once and if it doesn't work, I'm getting rid of you,' he said in the elevator.

The session seemed to have gone well, according to Mum's co-workers, who were pleased to see her and dad holding hands afterward, when they dropped into the childcare centre. Mum felt the session went really well and expressed she was sure the troubles in her marriage were going to be resolved. That knowledge was in contrast with my father's explanation for Mum's disappearance. He'd said she told him she needed space and was going to the Central Coast to get away. Why would Mum leave if she was so hopeful things were going to get better? It didn't make any sense – but not much did.

The failings of the police and the powers above were enormous, and highly suspicious in my opinion. In 1985, my Mum's friend and colleague Sue Strath wrote to the ombudsman to complain about the investigation – or lack thereof – into my Mother's disappearance. In her statement, she explained how J had been in a relationship with my father before Mum went missing, and how she'd moved into the family home. 'I've seen her on a Missing Person poster and I just cannot accept the explanation or reason of her whereabouts,' Sue wrote.

The reasons my father had given authorities didn't hold up. 'She needed time away from her husband.' Mum wouldn't have abandoned her marriage – or her family – the day after such a successful and hopeful counselling session. 'She ran away with a religious leader.' Mum wasn't religious and was obviously naively loyal to my father. 'She didn't love us anymore.' Bullshit.

The holes in my father's stories were gaping. But the authorities didn't investigate them. Police didn't interview Mum's friends, colleagues or neighbours. They didn't look into my father's (groomed) relationship with his student or his motives for getting rid of my Mother. Instead, the police took my father's word as gospel. They didn't pursue other leads. They let the case go cold.

In 2018, as the podcast was airing, my Auntie Pat wrote to the New South Wales Director of Public Prosecutions (DPP), as she had done multiple times before, about my Mother's case. She didn't get a reply.

Hedley Thomas's podcast highlighted so many issues around the investigation into my Mother's disappearance – the missing files, failure to follow through and dropped balls over the years make me want to hold people accountable. The screw-ups revealed in the podcast were infuriating to hear about.

Listening to my father's and other people's interviews with police, it was so obvious to me that there were so many things that didn't add up, so many blatant lies and things that should've been investigated and questioned more thoroughly at the time.

Hearing J's voice triggered me deeply. We heard about J's insistence that police should dig under the soft soil that was outside my bedroom window at our Bayview house. While driving around Bayview, J said to her friend, 'She's up there. She's somewhere up there on that block.'

'They haven't checked the soft soil,' J told her friend.

There were so many theories from so many different people shared in the podcast. One of them is that my Mother is still buried in our Bayview backyard, either deeper down under the cardigan they found or elsewhere on the property.

Another is that my Mother was buried in the backyard the night she disappeared and was then moved to another location.

I've had psychics tell me that my Mother's precious body isn't in one piece anymore. I don't have much hope that we'll find her body intact. I don't think we'll get the closure of burying her body whole. That's a brutal thing to try to come to terms with, though I still believe the whole truth might some day come to light. I am certain my father isn't the only one who knows exactly what happened.

The Teacher's Pet took on a life of its own. I like Hedley immensely as a person and hugely respect him as a journalist. I know he worked extremely long hours and at great personal expense to produce a captivating and popular podcast (and newspaper articles). He thoroughly deserves his hard-earned success and I will always be grateful that he gave me and my Mum's family a much-needed boost of hope and that he worked so hard trying to bring the truth to light. Hedley was the one who found the footage of my Mum on the *Chequerboard* program and I can't thank him enough for bringing her to us in that form. To see my Mother's grace, to see the way her eyes light up and crinkle when she smiles, to see her animated in a visual form once again was such an incredible gift.

As grateful as I am to Hedley for what he has done, it does not sit well with me that the company he works for has sold the rights for the production of a mini-series and made money entertaining the masses (as they do) with this story, while we're the ones who've been living the story. It is *my Mother's story!!!* It is my and my family's story. We've had to live it for forty fucking years. We didn't get paid for our interviews and, ironically, I couldn't even read the articles because I'm not a subscriber of the publication Hedley writes for. This is a major flaw in our news and entertainment industry as far as I'm concerned.

In what was meant to be the last episode of *The Teacher's Pet* before a well-earned break for the team, Hedley decided to end with my words. I read out the poem I wrote in 2018 titled 'Mother', which is included in the opening chapter of this book. That part of the podcast came to a close with the sentence: 'But a hole where a Mother should be, all I can do is breathe into where I long for her to be.'

When the podcast started, I could never have predicted the ripple effect it would have. I don't think anyone could have. Even after fourteen episodes, when the podcast wrapped for a break, we didn't know what would happen next. I was hopeful that the power of the podcast and pressure from the public would turn the wheels of justice in my Mother's case.

Hope is certainly a precious commodity and one which needs to be reignited continuously in situations like these and, simultaneously, a certain degree of ambiguity is also required because clinging to a hope that might not eventuate could certainly lead to gutting angst or, possibly, insanity.

I had by this point certainly hit a wall with regards to maintaining the pretence within my family. I simply couldn't do it anymore and I do regret not speaking with my sister about it in person, but I was so overcome with the grief and trauma that was being triggered, it was all I could do to pull it together enough to keep my daughter feeling relatively safe and comforted in her world. The podcast contributed to severing the gags that were binding and stifling me, only this time I wasn't walking away alone as I had in the numerous replayed scenarios in my mind. Now I have hundreds, thousands, of people walking beside me offering their condolences and sharing the belief that my father was guilty of murdering my Mother.

This is the last text I ever sent my father on Father's Day, the 2nd of September 2018 …

> **You are my father and I'll always love you; you are a part of me and me of you. But I won't live a life based on lies, nor will I keep subjecting myself to emotional manipulation and control.**
>
> **I love everyone in our family but have been observing for years how I'm treated differently, as though I'm inferior. It is so obvious, the lack of respect you all have for me. I will go where I feel valued and in relationships based on mutual respect.**

I have been battling with PTSD, depression and anxiety since traumatic childhood memories resurfaced a number of years ago.

You have dishonoured our Mother so terribly and also my sister and me through all of this. No more.

One day I will forgive you for removing her so selfishly from our lives. Perhaps one day you will take responsibility for your actions and the effect they've had on so many people, most of all your daughters and granddaughters. I hope that we can have a relationship based on truth, honour and compassion.

My father, Love always conquers.

He replied to me the same day:

Shanelle, I have started to write a reply to your very disturbing letter at least ten times. I need to be on the Gold Coast for at least one week. When I am able, I want to come up and see you and obviously have a much needed and overdue talk. Love as always Dad xx

And then again the next day ...

It took time to digest the hurtful message you sent, Shanelle, but you are clearly very lonely and depressed in the life you have chosen. This is not

about me. You have continuously pushed your family away and made the choice to be 'free spirited'. Shanelle, you chose to live with K and then other friends since you were seventeen. You were a very happy child and a strong-willed teenager who hung out with the cool kids. You were given lots of love and every opportunity to be what you wanted to be, and then chose it.

You travelled the world for fifteen of your twenty years of adult life and only returned because you were pregnant ... You know very little about what was going on in my life or Sherry's. It is your adult life, now forty-one with a child and without a partner, that has clearly caused this terrible depression. We all unfortunately have to live with the choices we make. I OWN my poor choices and you never need to remind me of them. You need to work out how you will move forward from here, but I would love my daughter back ... one who can live in the present and the future, and move forward from here. Love you both very much, Dad xx

I didn't reply. And my father didn't follow through by visiting for the 'long overdue talk' he had actually suggested on other occasions as well.

The last text message I received from my father was on the 11th of September 2018. It read ...

Hi Shanelle, hope you and Kialah are both well.

Thinking of you constantly xx

It was not in my nature to ignore him, but I didn't have the capacity to respond and didn't feel we were moving forward in truth, which was the only way to go, from my perspective.

We were still living in Hervey Bay when I was approached to do an interview with the current affairs program *60 Minutes*. I was interviewed in August and the episode aired later in 2018. As part of the filming, the producer organised for Kialah and I to go swimming with whales off Hervey Bay. The rule of thumb for whale watching is to let them come to you, so that's what we did. We were in the water, holding on to ropes connected to the boat, with two huge humpbacks swimming underneath us. One of the whales looked up at me curiously, and we made eye contact. I swear it looked me straight in the eye. It was the most profoundly peaceful and beautiful experience, they are the most magnificent creatures.

What came next was far from peaceful …

After the episode aired, my stepmother called and left a message on my voicemail. 'Well done, you got through it okay. You've known your father as a child for seventeen years, I've known him for twenty-five years as an adult. I *know* there's no way that he's capable of murdering your Mother,' she said. I felt a lot of compassion for her in this moment, I understood her disbelief and was worried for her, should the truth ever come out. I don't recall if I ever called her back; I don't think I did. I didn't stop caring, I just didn't know how to relate to her at all anymore, or how to engage in the situation with such different perspectives.

One family member accused me of 'selling out', which I was not, and after my participation in the podcast, another member of the family sent me an abusive email basically telling me I was a worthless piece of shit who contributed nothing to the family. I told this person that if they ever abused me again that I'd put out an AVO on them.

I'm assuming it was my decision to share my story that caused these relatives to block me, without any explanation. Or perhaps it had become apparent that I believed that it was my father who murdered my Mother, even though I refused to say so on national TV as I was still clinging to semblances of thin threads of relations with my sister. There was still a tiny part of me that hoped I was wrong and that what I thought were memories were actually misconstrued.

I think I understand, from a very black and white perspective, why my sister was mad with me. I assumed she felt me speaking publicly about our Mother was betraying my father, or perhaps she felt betrayed herself? But too many people accepting my father's version of my Mother's disappearance allowed him to get away with his crime for too long. Silence protects perpetrators.

I wonder if my sister got rid of any gifts I've given her and her children over the years? Just as our father made us do when J left and he turned her mother into a villain for taking her in. He made us send back everything she'd ever given. I understand the coping mechanism. To pretend the person never existed, remove any memory of them, so without the triggers it's easier to shove back down any projections of blame or hurt they've caused.

A few weeks after the podcast paused for a break, police vans pulled up outside my childhood home in Bayview. Officers started digging with shovels and heavy machinery, using new technology. They ripped up pavers and cut into the Earth. They dug into the ground; they dug into the past. I started to write while I gripped my phone, waiting for news, and wondering if they could even tell me if they found anything. I couldn't sleep, anxiety was high; deep breathing wasn't cutting it to bring calm and I was a complete mess. Here's what I wrote to attempt to channel my angst outside of myself:

A Poem

16th of September 2018
Hervey Bay, Queensland

Sunday night can't sleep, did you find my Mum?
The winds of change knock at the doors to my soul
My inner four-year-old child, rightfully angry
Takes centre stage, filled with rage
Lashes out
To keep the world at bay
Who to trust, no-one at most
Another player tries stepping in
But she has not felt heard
Her soul shattering roar
Heart wailing for her Mummy
For her daddy
How could he? How could he? NOOOOOOOOOOOOOOOO!!!!!!!!
I want my Mummy, but I still love you daddy.
Destructive explosive charge
Without a channel
Makes me go dead inside
Until I know how to deal with it
Bitter medicine
Transformed into gold
Alchemy for the soul
To expand and become whole
Calling fragments home
But first must banish
What stepped in, to fill the hole.

Holes dug to bury her deep
Love doesn't die but bodies and trust do
Funeral arrangements
Pregnant with child
Tears awaken, years of non-remembrance
Dissolving, cleansing, release ...
Food for the Earth rebirth
The Phoenix rising from the ashes of
Cremation
My dear Mother Always, loved.

CHAPTER TWELVE

The Elephant Occupying the Whole Bloody Room Comes Charging

In September 2018, a memorial walk was held along the headland at Long Reef on the Northern Beaches of Sydney on the weekend that would've been my Mother's seventieth birthday. People wore pink and carried pink flowers, symbolic of the pink cardigan found in the dig around the pool. Somewhere along the line, it must have been reported it was my Mother's favourite colour, but it was not – her favourite colour was blue. The walk was a lovely, honouring and unifying thing to do.

I was grateful to the people who organised the walk, and to everyone who showed up to honour my Mum; many who knew and loved her, but also strangers who felt moved by her story. I had a couple of people says things along the lines of, 'Don't worry, we'll get the bastard.' This hurt my heart and wasn't what the walk was about for me.

I appreciated being there, though I wasn't asked if I wanted to contribute anything, or if I wanted to speak, as Hedley and my uncle did. My Auntie Merilyn brought flowers for me to carry and organised a stroller for Kialah. Because my daughter doesn't walk in straight lines – or stay confined to a stroller – we lagged behind. My cousin stayed with us as we brought up the rear, which I was so thankful for.

When we finally arrived at the top of the hill, I shared a beautiful moment, hands and hearts momentarily linked, holding my Auntie Pat's arm close and feeling our mutual love for and loss of my Mum. We laid down our flowers for her together. Afterward, my other cousins played with my daughter so I could be off duty for a moment. Family support, what a lovely thing to experience.

The day was an overwhelming and indecipherable blur for me, though I'm sure the people present would understand. I remember beautiful music, hundreds of kind faces and a generous artist sketching a portrait of my Mother as a gift for the family. The outpouring of love, compassion and care for my Mother, but also especially for my sister (who didn't attend) and myself, was touching. These moments have held me up and held me close during waves of massive grief.

It was really strange to have the media there, photographing us in such a raw and vulnerable state, I can only hope it was to honour my Mum and not to be vulture-like.

The dig in Bayview didn't unearth anything, but even in the absence of a body, the police still had enough evidence to arrest my father.

On the 5th of December 2018, New South Wales police detectives flew to Queensland to arrest a 'known person' for the murder of my Mother, Lyn. The known person was my father, Chris. The image that stays in my head, as I recall that sad, sad day, is of my father wearing shorts and thongs and being escorted from his Gold Coast home by suit-wearing detectives. His head is bowed down. 'My dear dad,' I thought as I watched him being taken off to jail. 'I know you've done a *really* fucking horrible thing and this is necessary justice, but it still breaks my heart, again and again.'

I didn't write in my diary on the day my father was arrested.

If I remember correctly, I was sent a text from police just moments before the messages started pouring in from people who are more news savvy than me. I believe I managed to drop my daughter at kindy, then returned home. I closed all the curtains and slumped against a wall in the kitchen, alternating between shock and wailing in foetal position on the floor. Yes, I wanted the truth, but it was still completely excruciating.

I received a lot of messages on my phone, a number of them requesting interviews, but I was in no state to talk, or think or do anything. I was so grateful there were no reporters knocking on my door. Silence, sensory insulation, is the only saviour during such deep processing for me.

Twelve days after my father's arrest, he was granted bail with 'strict conditions'. The conditions included good behaviour, daily reporting to the police station near his home on the Sunshine Coast, $1.5 million in surety, and no contact at all with anyone who had made a statement to police.

My father might have been out of jail, but none of us were free. I often thought of my family, and especially my sister, and wondered how she was coping. I assumed she probably still believed our father was innocent, and I wondered if any circumstantial evidence would ever be enough to convince her otherwise? In the weeks and months after my father was charged with my Mother's murder, I struggled and fell apart, yet again.

It was quite a shock to me when around Christmas, there was a knock on the door. I wasn't expecting anybody and am rarely up for visitors at the best of times, so I hid and waited. There was a package left for my daughter, from my father and stepmother. Nothing for me, but some gifts and a lovely card for Kialah. I was really confused by this and questioned my father's motives … I was assuming at this point that my father hadn't shared my text with my stepmother. My daughter and I moved back to the Sunshine Coast hinterland shortly after this.

A Series of Diary Entries

28th of March 2019
Sunshine Coast Hinterland, Queensland

When all physical security is stripped away, the challenge is not to go into fight or flight, but can we stand firm in our connection to the divine? In that space when eyes are closed and nothing exists except Great Spirit … can we carry that deep knowing into our everyday world.

2nd of May 2019
Sunshine Coast, Queensland

Lately I'm finding myself being really manic. I have a few psychics helping tune into where my Mother is buried. I'm questioning whether I'm being obsessive and neurotic by needing to know where she is but the need to have her all to myself one last time before sharing her with the world, runs deep. I feel myself as part of the greater whole. My soul's purpose, though only a ghostly whisper of it, steers me in a direction that resonates with conviction in my body's wisdom. So I have vague impressions and the nagging intuition these women are on the right track and I'm waiting for more solid information to come to me, or even the impulse to act. I get impatient frequently but I also trust my instincts and sense of timing.

Truth will always come to light eventually. My Mother's story is finally being heard and in between the lines are the stories of so many others who have shared a similar, tragic fate. Our society needs a massive overhaul; no wonder our foundations are crumbling. Systems that are not in truth and integrity can't sustain themselves.

I remember reading the statistics for how many women have experienced domestic violence and/or sexual abuse at some point in their lives and thinking that's an awful lot of people being abused, and an awful huge number of people abusing. Has it always been this high throughout history or is our society becoming more ill? How do we get to the root of this problem and begin to eradicate it? It's so important that the people doing the abusing get help and support too, because they won't feel safe to step forward and ask for help when there is so much shame and stigma attached nor will they receive the healing they need and the cycles perpetuate.

3rd of May 2019
Sunshine Coast, Queensland

Some people might have the perception that my choosing not to confront my father once I came to know/remember the truth was a sign of weakness. It wasn't. It was the gentlest path for myself, my mental health and my ability to continue to mother my child without having a complete breakdown. I didn't want to lose my sister, though inevitably I've lost her anyway. At least I have more general support behind me now, with this later departure. Being an orphan is quite lonely at times, though I often felt like that even when I was still in the family. I've never really fit in or

felt understood, nor could I relate to them and what I think of as
superficial ways. Our priorities are different, shall we say? I feel a
lot of grief for my child, with no cousins, father, siblings, aunties,
uncles or grandparents. I can only pray one day we'll be adopted
into a soul family and feel a sense of belonging and live with people
who are as invested in our well–being, as we are in theirs.

Not confronting the truth about my father was a survival instinct. For years, I was mentally preparing myself and rehearsing how I would do it. I wanted to go about it in the gentlest way for my siblings and stepmother – and myself. I considered if it was best to send them letters directly, or to just send my father one and let him relay the information. I felt a sense of responsibility to them in sharing the truth. Although, I probably should have realised that they wouldn't have believed me and prepared myself for the likelihood that I would be abused for saying that my father had murdered my Mother. There were so many multi-faceted reasons I didn't say it out loud for such a long time.

On the night of Father's Day 2019, a year after I texted my final words to my father, I dreamed of him. In the dream, he was his kind, gentle part of himself; the aspect of him that my Mother loved and married. My Dad. He said, 'Hi darl,' in an affectionate tone. Part of me still loved that part of him. That can be so incredibly confusing: still loving someone who you also despise.

The world sees a monster, but I see my dad. Despite it all, I still love him. The love I have felt for him for forty-one years doesn't simply dissipate because of what he's done. It's much more complicated than that.

Sometimes I'll hear a song that we used to sing together, windows down, driving along happily, and the song will take me back to another time. A time before I stopped calling my father 'dad', before I came to know the truth. Before my bubble burst and my heart was shattered into thousands of tiny, broken pieces. My soul is still intact, not even he can touch that, but attempting to mend my heart has been a journey.

When a child has trust broken by their parents or primary caregivers, it ripples out into every relationship and is really difficult to restore. Emotionally, I don't truly trust anybody except myself. Though I'm working on restoring that trust in people again.

In seeing my father for who he really is, I didn't just lose him, I also lost my sister and his side of the family. I still wonder, does my sister miss me? Does she miss my daughter, her niece? I've lost a lot through all of this, but I just wanted answers about what happened to our beautiful Mother. I want her life to matter, her memory to be honoured and the truth to be told about her.

The divisions within my family pain me. It's not just on my father's side either. When I tried to talk to some of my Mother's family years ago about the incident with the grandfather when I was a child, their reactions were immediately dismissive. They weren't supportive or believing of me.

It wasn't an easy subject to breach – especially when I was already feeling a bit raw from other family upheavals and being ostracised.

They doubted my recollections because they were a 'bit vague'. They said Pa wouldn't do something like that because 'he was very proper'. Well, fuck proper.

Maybe he was going senile, and it was not in his usual character, but I also remember him making inappropriate comments to the nurses who were coming to bandage his toes due to diabetes … That wasn't 'proper'! Nanna would 'tsk tsk', shake her head and call him a 'dirty old sod'.

The reason my recollections of Pa's actions might have come across as vague (the other reason for not believing me) was because I spoke gingerly to soften the blow, and my memories did creep back in like a thick fog. I was unsure of what the reaction would be, and it seems my concerns were founded. I'm not softening the blow to my own detriment anymore. I'm sorry, Nanna, I know you asked me not to tell anyone, but I won't be silenced anymore.

In order to heal and create a better world, these things need to stop being swept under the carpet and need to be properly addressed. I don't know how we get to the root of these problems, to dissolve the predatory entitlement some people have over accessing another human without their consent and with no regard to the effect it has on them.

As a woman with sexual abuse in my past, it has taken me a long time to identify (on much more subtle levels) that the value I hold goes so much deeper and wider than whether or not I am offering my body for sex and the types of men that don't see my value beyond that. I believe the statistics state one in four women have experienced some form of sexual abuse at some point in their lives. No, it's not all men, but that is a lot of men and this needs to change. Yes, I'm aware it's women who can be perpetrators too, but the numbers of abuse by men are significantly higher (perhaps because of physical strength and a patriarchal society?) and I'm talking based on my own personal experiences. It's awkward and difficult to talk about these things, and I understand why many prefer to stay in ignorance.

Or maybe it hasn't affected them personally and therefore doesn't hold as much relevance. Well, it does affect every single one of us in one way or another. Whether it's how your mother and father relate (or mother and mother, father and father etc), or how your sister doesn't feel safe to walk home alone at night, or even how male caregivers can be looked at with more suspicion, or preference given to a female to fill the role. Unfortunately, I have done this too, based on my own experiences. I don't mistrust all men, but nor will I take the risk with my own daughter, feeling that the risks outweigh the benefits. There's so much pain in the world, it's hard to know where to start to make things better. Empathy and open discussions are very good starting points.

A Poem

November 2019
Sunshine Coast, Queensland

Stillness washes over me
Moves through me like an oceanic blanket of peace
Reaching extremities of mind
Bringing me back to my heart
This is how I feel safest where harshness can't harm
Stillness. Sweet, sweet friend
Nothingness and everything
Where is my Mother?

CHAPTER THIRTEEN

Where is My Mother?

Two psychics told me that they feel there is a remnant of my Mother's body to be found east of Glen Innes in country New South Wales. It didn't make logical sense that it would be so far from Bayview, but since two said the same thing, I went to explore the area in 2020. I thought it might have been possible that a route including Glen Innes was taken on the way to South West Rocks to pick up J. And it also may have been possible that there was help with disposing of my Mother's sacred body and this is where they took her.

My visit to the area was during a time of extreme drought and bushfires; the oppression was as thick in the air as the extreme, dry, stinking heat. Sections of the New England Highway were closed due to a fire, so I chose a route on the old highway, which I figured is what would have existed in 1982 anyway. As I drove across a particular bridge, a feeling of familiarity tickled my senses and gave me a bit of a nudge. There was someone camped or fishing down in the spot I felt drawn to, so I decided to keep driving. I half-heartedly looked around a dried creek bed, but it felt futile, and my daughter demanded my constant attention, which made it hard to tune in and feel my own intuition. Obviously, Kialah didn't know what we were doing; I probably told her we were looking for crystals in the rocks. Hard to make something so sinister feel like a fun game. The locals still waved, though the despair was palpable, their crushed spirits were heavy and their hope evaporated, just like the dried-up dams everywhere. We saw a dead cow, which brought home even more vividly the devastation the locals were experiencing. We sent love to the lands, the people and its animals as we drove around, praying for rain, for relief. I felt energy in a few spots, though I didn't know what that meant. My daughter fell asleep and it was too hot to leave her in the car, so I aborted the mission with the intention to return in the future.

I had by this point returned to the majestic lands of the Northern Rivers, which I deeply love. I had felt really sad leaving our dear friends on the Sunshine Coast, but it had never felt like home to me, as beautiful as those lands are. Each time I went to the coast, I would have panic attacks at the thought of seeing my father. When my father's bail conditions were changed, increasing his permitted radius of travel, this extended to the hinterland where we were living and I no longer felt emotionally safe, so that was the impetus for yet another home upheaval.

A Diary Entry

19th of May 2020
Northern New South Wales

Sometimes to step outside in a raw, vulnerable state feels overwhelming. Each sound, colour and movement assaults my senses. I'm hyper alert, fight or flight, a car sounds like a fighter jet. I can't calm my nervous system with my precious child talking at me constantly. She doesn't seem to need stillness as I do. It's not her fault, or mine. All the things I need, food, water, wee, clean, all the 'should do lists', all the people I haven't called back, swim in my mind all at once. I can't put them in chronological order. There are no straight lines to follow, just a fuzzy brain drowning in sensory overload. How many others feel like this regularly?

A Poem

16th of January 2021
Northern New South Wales

Dedicated to my beautiful friend, Dawn.
We walk side by side on opposite sides of the world,
navigating our way back to our true North.

No more chaotic, trauma distilled love
I want clear, Pacha Mama grounded, sky God inspired Love
Away from recycled playlists of outdated programs
Will he pave new roads with me?
Keen hawk eyes and full presence, to prevent the downward
spiral abyss of the past, that has long been so familiar
I am terrified to my human core, but it is only here
I can reach deeper into the unknown of
Safety that has existed within, though
not handed to me ancestrally.
Our compasses all spinning here on Earth
As we trust our hearts, our true north
To lead us HOME.

Months turned into years without a trial date in sight. We were all going through the Covid fucking nightmare. I was having lots of dread-laden dreams and disturbed sleep. I dreamed of a large wave and a dark shadow and heard myself call out 'Shark!'. I dreamed of locking my doors and my cousins looking for me, angry at me. I dreamed of a horse with no legs dying outside my home. I dreamed of my auntie wanting to keep her husband's phone and not letting the police have it. I dreamed I found footage of both my uncle and my father holding hands with my Mum in the shopping centre.

I had a really intense dream of a friend and her daughter, so I wonder if it was my Mother, father and me and my subconscious mind substituted? The dream was centred around a round pine dining table and resulted in an argument, brutal violence and lots of blood … When I returned to the scene, it had been cleaned up and furniture moved around for a fresh start. I was lucid enough to know I saw what happened, but when I woke, my mind had blocked the actual incident, more a knowing that I remembered.

More dark dreams, this time of a man pulling cars and car parts out of a lake/estuary/connected to ocean. I could see Sydney in the distance and was asking in my lucid state, if this was connected to my Mum and finding her remains? Unfortunately, I woke up without an answer.

Once I was awake, I wondered if I was in any danger, if there was more to the story of my Mother's murder? There certainly seems to have been corruption back then and cover-ups in the police force. If my father sought the assistance of another shady character, I certainly wouldn't want to dip my foot into that underworld.

A Dream

13th of September 2021
Northern New South Wales

I'm lying by a lake or a pond in the park, on a yoga mat
and am naked. I notice some people walking a trail and
realise it's my stepmother. She's joined to two other people.
I'm anxious about seeing her then my sister appears behind
me in a picnic chair. I'm trying to hide the fact I'm naked
and really hoping she wouldn't recognise me. We make
eye contact for a moment; I'm super anxious now.

In my car, it starts rolling backwards toward
her and I quickly pull the handbrake in time,
mortified. I try to give a little wave, indicating it
was intentional and I knew she was there.

I feel anxious with hints of shame, even though
I know I've done nothing wrong!

A Diary Entry

13ᵗʰ of October 2021
Northern New South Wales

What does my inner four-year-old psyche remember? What did she witness on that devastating night, the 8ᵗʰ of January 1982 ... the last time she saw her beautiful Mother alive? I can feel the weight of these memories; they make it difficult to move forward under such a heavy burden. My breathing is restricted. I wish to be free from this crushing weight.

It is NOT my fault my Mother was killed; I could not stop him.

Release. Any. Guilt. It is not mine.

Release ...

On the 24ᵗʰ of April 2022, I returned to the national parks east of Glen Innes, this time on my own thanks to the support of beautiful friends who offered to take care of Kialah for me. A rare bit of 'respite'. I drove out to Old Glen Innes Road again to look for my Mother's remains. I questioned whether I was delusional to even believe it was possible to find anything forty years later and with so little physical proof to act on, but I felt like I must. The magnetic force drew me along this road to certain spots. Perhaps nobody but 'God' will ever know why?

Beside mountain streams and under vast stars with no mobile reception or distractions to cloud my perception, I dreamed of my father, stepmother, siblings and our children.

The dream had a dark, damp basement feel of the deep subconscious.

We were at an amusement park and the kids were tired. Dad told us to wait, as there were only two rides and the tour of Sydney to go. I muttered something about being unenthused by concrete and bright city lights. My father was excited like a little boy to relive his childhood memories. My stepmother said sardonically, 'Aren't you excited to relive your happy childhood memories?' To which I replied, 'No, my childhood was shit!' I expected backlash for my honesty but surprisingly found none. The movie began, which immediately zoomed into someone blasting out another person's brains with a gun. I noted specific detail: the splats of blood had clumps in them. I immediately whisked my daughter off to bed, disgusted that my father thought this was appropriate for their young eyes. My siblings stayed, not wanting to offend my father and I prayed for the kids not to be too damaged by the exposure.

The time between my father's arrest and his trial was a hundred lifetimes: three years, five months, and four days. It was a torturous suspense. Not long before the trial eventually started, my daughter and I were struggling to find long-term housing in Northern New South Wales as a result of the severe flooding, and it was an extremely tumultuous time in our lives. Kialah and I joined thousands of others in homelessness. Thankfully, we moved from a campervan into a five-week sublet for the beginning of the trial, and I was super grateful to have the comforts of a home to emotionally process from.

A Poem

February 2022
Northern New South Wales

Nightmares and grief
Flooding lands coincide
With my eyes
Hearts walls gush
No control
Align with trust
And greater Grace
So we can finally
Know our place
Paving new roads
From flight to divine
Belonging
Safety
Love

The trial started in May 2022, and it lasted for ten weeks, with Justice Ian Harrison as the judge. I don't know if it was fitting or sickening that the trial started the day after Mother's Day. It all felt surreal to me, after waiting so long for my father to be arrested, and then for the trial to begin. When the police charged my father with murder, Hedley's podcast *The Teacher's Pet* had to be taken down until after a judgement was made. When the trial started, he covered it in a new podcast, *The Teacher's Trial*.

As the moon reached fullness, witnesses began being called.

I didn't write in my journal much during the trial; it was all consuming, and the longest ten weeks of my life. The Crown's case against my father presented three coexistent motives:

One of them was to get rid of Lynette Dawson. The second was to 'bring in J'. The third was to avoid the financial consequences of going through the Family Court and dissolving the marriage with Lynette Dawson.

Hearing these motives was sickening. What a shameful, unnecessary waste of a precious life.

I had intended on being at the trial in person for part of it, but I ended up listening to the entire thing via video link for various reasons – the main one being that I didn't have anyone to watch my daughter for me so I could attend. I felt a strong resentment at the situation, because surely I had more right to be there than most people. Paradoxically, it was probably in my best interest not being there. I suspect it would've been too much for me being in the courtroom; hearing it from the safety of my 'own space' was intense and traumatic enough as it was.

I tuned into the trial every day, trying to listen to every word, without Kialah hearing. At that point, she didn't know what the trial was about; I told her it was to do with my Mum, but she had no knowledge of her grandfather's direct involvement. I tried to maintain routine and as much normalcy for her as possible; meanwhile my insides were being ripped out and my head a whirling mess. As if that wasn't difficult enough, we then caught Covid. Luckily, we both had extremely mild cases but being in isolation together and meeting all of our needs for more than two weeks made tuning into the trial all day without Kialah hearing a complete nightmare.

Mid-trial, my daughter and I moved to another temporary space. Unfortunately this rental came with a beautiful but senile cat who most days pissed and pooped on the floor, couches and our suitcase and clothes! I spent my days madly trying to clean, before settling into the trial! Life is certainly never boring; but I really understand how people do go completely insane sometimes. It was added stress I really didn't need. I felt like I was teetering between the realms and walking a tight rope between them most of the time.

I felt fucked up, but I had every right to feel that way. It was understandable. What puzzled me was how my father ended up the way he is. What level of being mollycoddled and over-pampered makes a person as entitled as he is? Is *that* why he worked so hard to avoid my stepbrother being 'over-mothered', because he knew the damage that it had created for him? Though if my father is truly narcissistic – as some have suggested – he wouldn't own or be able to see that he is. Apparently, narcissism is not born, it is created. Is he truly a narcissist or is he just displaying narcissistic qualities? Was my father abused by someone? If so, who? He seems to have sex addiction, obsessive-compulsive and codependent behaviours – how were these created in his mind? So many questions and in trying to comprehend my father's actions, too many sleepless nights.

A Poem

28th of June 2022
Northern New South Wales

I'm so tired fight, flight, fawn and freeze!
Yet again, sleep disturbances
How much adrenaline
Fatigue
Can one nervous system measure
Too much for many lifetimes
This one
Needs stop
Restore
No more slowly killing me
Like you did, my Mother
The Wade versus Roe law overturned
My anger is churning
For men like my father
To believe they are entitled to
Power over another
Women's bodies
Misogynistic views
Take two
Your Jekyll and Hyde horror runs over
The power lies within
Gives rise to ripe action
Tides turning
Dominant systems crumble
RIP we say

It was brutally confronting to hear the stories again, of my Mother's bruises and my father's abuse. I cried a lot. There was one witness who relayed a memory of my Mother and her, realising at the time that they were astral travelling simultaneously and had seen each other in the lucid dreaming process. I found this very beautiful, as I had no idea my Mother was into that kind of thing. It angered me that the defence was belittling and trying to make this lovely woman out to be crazy. She held her own in a calm and matter-of-fact manner. I wondered why the Crown didn't protect her more from that, but was grateful I got to hear this precious little element of my dear Mum. I got to hear my Mum's job application for her childcare job, hear her hobbies and see her writing. This was precious. I love hearing people recall how lovely she was … tragically bittersweet.

When J took the stand, it was confronting for me to see her for the first time since she left us – this woman who wore my Mother's shoes but never filled them. I felt a lot of compassion for her. It couldn't have been easy for her to relive the past and have such personal details aired so publicly – especially since she has chosen to be very private since the beginning. It must have been extremely uncomfortable to sit there and be forced to listen to every word of love letters my father had written to her as a teenager being read out for all to hear. That room must have felt akin to a torture chamber. J was really courageous in the way she held her own. I sincerely hoped that she wasn't affected too badly by it all and that the trial would bring her some closure and help concrete it in the past.

Some days were harder than others. I often felt frustrated and angered at the 'justice' system and its flaws. When I learned that two particular witnesses were giving evidence via video link, I couldn't believe it. I believe they are two people who know the truth of what happened! The fact that they were not being held accountable and having to face court was a complete cop-out, utter bullshit. Why were they not under the same fierce scrutiny the defence barrister inflicted on innocent witnesses who were telling the truth?!

The whole ordeal was so one-sided. The system and those involved let my Mother down at the time of her murder, and yet again it was the victims of crime who were left to suffer the damage and consequences of the faulty system, rather than the perpetrators. The fact that the accused – my father – didn't have to take the stand was unbelievable to me. People who were not being accused, innocent witnesses, had no choice in the matter. They had to put their whole lives on hold as they went through the gruelling process of attending court and retelling their memories. And yet, my father could sit there silently. Each time I heard blatant, over-rehearsed lies being told under oath, I yelled at my phone and was certain I would've been told to leave the courtroom had I been there.

Two months into the trial, I heard my father's defence team use what I said in my *60 Minutes* interview about him being a good dad as evidence to support his good character. That caused me so much pain and anxiety – that my words could be used in support of him and without my permission.

I couldn't listen to the proceedings on those last weeks because my mental health had taken a steep dive and I was also badly triggered by his barrister. I remembered my father's barrister from when she represented him during his bitter custody battle with J. I recall her visiting our house at Coomera and that my father asked her on a date, but she declined! The way the defence is allowed to talk to witnesses so horribly and can say whatever they want, to accuse witnesses of lying, is another way the process is one-sided. Whilst the Crown has to submit each question and have it 'approved' beforehand. The way the defence caused suffering to innocent witnesses – felt cruel.

The comments I made on *60 Minutes* about my father were in the context of the fact he wasn't physically abusive toward us children and he was in some ways a good dad over the years; but I was also being overly diplomatic in the interview because I was attempting to honour my Mum and keep my sister.

Not being in the courtroom, I felt removed, forgotten and irrelevant.

A Diary Entry

31st of August 2022
Northern New South Wales,
In a slightly longer-term home (finally)

The verdict came through yesterday, just after three o'clock. It took five hours to be delivered and I was gripping my phone tightly all day, glued to every word the judge said. What a roller-coaster ride that was. I was grateful the lovely victim support lady had warned me of this; it certainly helped me ride the waves with a lot less internal friction. My phone reception was wavering in and out at times, torturing me further. I sat by the river for some time, she soothed me, but it felt surreal as I watched other people happy in their daily lives, while this massive thing was unfolding in mine.

As the judge rejected certain pieces of evidence that I very much believed to be true, an understanding arose within that he was being very specific with what he was allowing in so that his verdict was watertight and leaving no grounds for appeal. It felt like that comfort was offered to me by my Mother, who I felt strongly with me the whole day. She would have been with all of her loved ones simultaneously, as she is not bound by time and space limitations as we are on Earth.

I had to collect my daughter from her bush school at three, with the judge still talking through the speaker on my phone. Somehow I had to put on a smile and brave face for her, trying to work out how I could still listen but keep its revealings from her ears and understanding. Just at that moment as we walked home, my beautiful angel friend, dressed in white, came walking across the *bridge toward us, her children in tow, and offered to take my daughter for the afternoon. Bless you, thank you, yes!!! She knew what was happening and had tried to message me, but of course I wasn't checking messages once court began.*

'I am satisfied beyond reasonable doubt that the Crown has proved the single count in the indictment,' Justice Harrison found. 'Christopher Michael Dawson, on the charge that on or about 8 January 1982 at Bayview or elsewhere in the State of New South Wales you did murder Lynette Joy Dawson, I find you guilty.'

The judge was brilliant, concise, highly perceptive and definitely a mastermind, in my opinion.

I went into shock and disassociation, which was a surprising reaction to knowing one way or the other what was coming. I heard the clank of handcuffs, that sound would keep repeating in my head. I could only see the judge from my live-streamed front seat. I wish I could've seen my dad and been in the courtroom in my right-down-the-middle, mixed feelings of despair and relief.

Many people celebrated the news and sent me congratulations. I was not there with them; there was no part of me that felt a celebration was appropriate for my own process. There was no rejoicing.

I was glad that the truth had finally come out, for I knew it would help set my Mother free from the lies and polluting of her essence. Justice has been done; this was a necessary part of the journey and I accept it as such. It was a large dose of closure, at last. It brought more healing than I realised it would, to have that guilty verdict. I was trying to remain unattached to the outcome, to prevent further grief for myself, if a verdict of guilty had not been returned.

I was still in shock when I went to pick up my daughter from the park. A baby bird had fallen out of its nest and the children were squabbling over whose turn it was to hold it. Maternal and protective instincts kicked in. The others all left, and my daughter and I stood in the approaching dark, light rain misting us as we stood on watch, guardians of the baby bird while we waited for a volunteer from WIRES to come. It felt very metaphorical somehow and certainly prompted the need for me to stay present and more fully embodied. The bird obviously felt safe with my daughter and hopped over to where she was sitting, into her lap and up to her shoulder. This made us giggle and was a heart-warming moment, alongside the other big feelings that were largely on pause until I could get my daughter to bed.

In Sydney, outside the courthouse where the guilty verdict had been delivered, my Uncle Greg read out a statement …

This is a verdict for Lynette.

Today her name has been cleared – she loved her family and never left them of her own accord. Instead, her trust was betrayed by the man she loved.

Shanelle Dawson

The court has found what we have believed to be true for so many years, that Chris Dawson took the life of our beloved Lyn back in 1982.

On behalf of Lyn's family, heartfelt thanks to all who came forward to speak truth for Lyn, to give Lyn a voice forty years after she lost her own. Many of those people have been advocating for Lyn for a very long time.

And thanks to those in the media who allowed those voices to speak loudly; missing people need to be heard despite their own voices being silent.

Thank you to those police and prosecutors who saw the truth of Lyn's story, and pulled various disjointed facts into a cohesive whole.

We'd also like to acknowledge Justice Harrison who made it plain that he was across the evidence put to him.

We acknowledge the difficulty this outcome will cause for some; we hope in time that understanding will lead to healing.

We also would like to remember those who loved Lyn who are not here to see this judgement, in particular Helena and Len Simms, and Phil Simms.

This is a milestone in our journey of advocating for Lyn.

However, the journey is not complete.

Lyn is still missing; we still need to bring her home.

**We would ask Chris Dawson to find it in himself
to finally do a decent thing, and allow us to bring
Lyn home to a peaceful rest, finally showing her the
dignity she deserves.**

It was some days later when I emerged ever slightly from my cave of stillness, just enough to write this in my diary, though I couldn't muster the capacity to share it publicly by putting it on my Facebook page at the time, it became a much more abbreviated version …

Dear kind people,

**Thank you so much for all of your messages of love
and support. I so deeply appreciate them. My feelings
are too big to add anything else yet. I'm processing
in the way that works for me, in deep stillness, by
allowing myself to feel everything. I will re-emerge
from my cave once the feelings aren't drowning me.
I've read every single message and they have been
gentle balm for my hurting heart.**

**But I will rise up again, as I have many times before.
Thank you.**

It took a long time to process the guilty verdict. Weeks after the ruling, I dreamed of two particular family members. I was with them and they were talking to someone outside the car window. They were how they used to be; the people I used to love.

Later, I dreamed of my stepmother. She was warm toward me, which surprised me, and I noticed she was disassociated or heavily sedated. She told me, 'Have your father call me.' To which I slightly awkwardly replied, 'I'm not speaking to him at the moment' and waited for her reaction. She just went vague and chatted about nonsensical things.

In my dream – and in reality – I felt really sorry for my sister and stepmother. The verdict must have been a massive shock to her. As it must have been for many others on my father's side. In the days following the trial, I thought of my sister often and hoped she was okay.

The sentencing hearing was scheduled for the 10th of November 2022, which was the day after the full moon and lunar eclipse. I battled with the decision whether to go to Sydney to deliver my victim impact statement in person in court. I started having panic attacks at the thought of seeing my father – and yet I knew it was the most optimal choice for my own healing journey. I knew seeing my father in custody was going to be heartbreaking for me, and being in the same room as the Dawson family would be so vastly confronting and trauma triggering. I hoped that they would organise to have my father out of prison garb.

I would have much preferred to stay in my safe bubble, but I knew it was something I must do to further bring about closure for myself and claim back the power that was taken from me.

A Diary Entry

1st of November 2022
Northern New South Wales

Memories all locked away in a room in my mind, a padded cell, for if they escaped all together I'd certainly go completely insane. Frustrating to feel them locked away and inaccessible to me, though I trust in the wisdom of my body with the knowing that I'm not ready. So as survival would have it, they are allowed to escape small snippets at a time. Until I got hypnotherapy, that unleashed big memories, confusion, doubt that they are real memories as I attempt to shove them back into the armed fortress of my mind. Forget that they tried to escape.

I have invited all memories to come out now I feel strong enough to chance the marathon of them. I don't want to feel the weight bearing on my soul, infiltrating into the freedom that is my and all of our birthright. I want to feel joy again.

251

CHAPTER FOURTEEN

I Am Of My Mother

Growing up, I had this perception of my father as a bit of a goody-two-shoes. He didn't drink or smoke, had never tried pot (I mean come on, he was a youth in the sixties and seventies!), and listened to what I thought of as squeaky-clean music such as the Bee Gees, The Hollies. 'He Ain't Heavy, He's My Brother' was a sentimental song for him and his twin brother. It made him light up, all the catchy music with great harmonies, and I loved that stuff too. We used to turn it up, windows down, and sing every word together (that was, until his third wife came along – then it was no music, windows up, air con on).

As an adult, I remember watching *Jersey Boys* with my dad in his Sunshine Coast home; his face lit up when his favourite 'golden oldies' were playing, and he was singing along with the enthusiasm of an eager boy. Their preppy and polished image rapidly dissolved for me, as the reality of what really went on backstage became apparent … And the irony of the superficial act I was engaged in with my father, just to keep the illusion of peace and my sister, though in reality, these had both been lost long ago.

The night before my father's sentencing for the murder of my Mother, I watched *Jersey Boys*. I cried at the song 'Sherry', which was always my sister's song growing up and reminds me of seemingly happier times. That night, I mourned deeply the father I once thought I knew, but I also remembered how I felt disgusted, when in the movie Johnny was being an arsehole to the ladies and my father laughed. The misogyny made me want to vomit and start a revolution.

It had been a nauseating and rebellion-inducing few weeks. On the 9th of November 2022, I gratefully dropped my daughter off with our lovely friends and drove to the airport where I would board a flight to Sydney to deliver my victim impact statement. The trip almost felt as though I was marching toward my own execution. Just after take-off on my flight south, a rainbow appeared in the clouds over the ocean and then a second one, suspended in the sky to the left of the plane. It was one of the brightest and most spectacular rainbows I've ever seen! I'd never seen anything like that before. Animated refractions of light and changing angles caused it to do all sorts of magical looking arcs and it appeared to be following the plane! I felt the support of my Mother and Spirit with me in that moment. I looked around to see if anybody else was witnessing the rainbow and feeling as much awe and amazement as me, but the people on the plane seemed oblivious and most were looking down at their screens. I'm not one to take many photos, but I really regretted that my phone was in the overhead locker!

On the day of the court hearing, I stepped out onto the busy Sydney street and the sound of traffic assaulted my ears. The buses and people and noise – a hive of activity that some people thrive in – stung my skin and hurt my ears and senses. When the concrete to tree ratio is out of balance, I feel like I'm suffocating. The city pace and rat race mentality, along with the pollution, thickens the air to further compound the feeling of asphyxiation for me.

I braced myself, as if facing a blizzard … to go and get breakfast! God help me for the actual court hearing, I thought. On a normal day, I'd find navigating my way through public transport and in a city challenging. But with what I was preparing to do, it was completely daunting. Thankfully, my lovely friend had left her family to fend for themselves and came to Sydney to support me. She brought her grounded practicality and sharp intelligence with her caring heart.

En route to the New South Wales Supreme Court, I took deep breaths and clutched the lavender I picked from a footpath garden to help me relax and for nature to soothe me, as I knew I would find the confinements of the courtroom stifling. I wished I had thought to bring something of my Mother's to hold and to feel her more tangibly with me. At the same time, I realised I have myself and I am of my Mother!

I'm sure she was there with me every step of the way. I felt our shared strength and determination as I faced my father, her husband, her killer – on her behalf and my own.

When my father was brought into the courtroom, I started to cry at the sight of him. As he limped toward his chair, in his prison greens, the tears kept coming. What I needed in that moment was a full-body throw-myself-to-the-ground wail. Unfortunately, those of us from a British heritage, who carry remnants of its prim and proper culture, are not allowed such raw and honest expressions of feelings in public. I shoved the grief back down except for an excusable and understandable sob, which I couldn't completely contain.

Obviously it was heartbreaking, but also beautiful to see and feel the support for my Mother and our family in the courtroom. To hear the statements of Mum's remaining brother and sister read out in court was soul-wrenchingly painful. But it was also (at least for me) powerful to see them get the opportunity to honour her, to be heard and witnessed in their love and loss of her. It made it feel possible to move through those hurting parts in a more direct way. Perhaps the love those parts received, once they were brave enough to be vulnerable and exposed, would help them settle in peace and find their rightful place, no longer needing to scream their existence in order to be accepted and loved.

I felt touched by the beauty and the grief upon hearing my auntie and uncle express their love for my Mum and snippets of their childhood memories.

During the reading of my auntie and uncle's statements, my father sat facing the judge, never once acknowledging or showing any remorse for what was being spoken.

There were letters of support for my father too – including ones written by my sister, half-sister and my father's wife – but they weren't read out loud in court. The judge read them on his own.

As I approached the bench, my father turned his body to look at me, his movement unnatural and reptilian-like. It was reported in the media that I stared fiercely at my father. This is not true.

He stared at me, and I held my own, with compassion, sorrow and consciously calling home any power that he has taken from me throughout my life. Courtrooms need serious energy clearings! There's so much dense and stuck energy in there!

My internal dialogue was as such ... 'Oh fuck, this is intense. Is he trying to say sorry through his stare? No, I don't think so ... is he trying to intimidate me?'

'I'm sure if he is truly a narcissist, then he will blame me in part, for his demise.'

'Oooooh fuck, how long do we keep this up for? Oh no, I came here to dissolve entanglements, not to allow further psychic cords to attach to me!!!'

I called on my angels and spirit guides to keep me safe and protected from any energetic attacks from my father. I don't remember who broke the gaze, though I'm told it was him, and I started reading my statement. The fluorescent lights were excessively bright and loud to my senses. I was initially aware of everyone in the room, but once I sat down, it was just him and me. It felt surreal.

As I was reading, my father turned to the side and I noticed very subtle shakes of his head at some of what I was saying; one of those things being how he took family dinners and loving grandparents away from my child. This showed me that at least he was listening, even if he didn't appear to be.

I wanted to yell at him in those moments, 'What, don't you agree???!!! Well, it's true, you fucking arsehole!!!'

It took a lot of energy to restrain myself, as I assumed I would be kicked out of court. It took almost an hour to read my statement out loud, I'm told. While I was reading, I was in a zone where I was oblivious to time and all else except my father. I blocked out the other faces in the room; I didn't hear the gasps or see the tears. Somehow, I made it through my entire statement without combusting into flames. Here is what I said, directly to my father …

MY VICTIM IMPACT STATEMENT

The night you removed our Mother from our lives, was the night you destroyed my sense of safety and

belonging in this world for many decades to come. Almost all of the love, nurturing and kindness vanished from my life.

Because of your selfish actions, we will never see her again, we will never hear her tell us she loves us, feel her hold us or hear her laugh.

There are not enough words in the English language to describe the impact of forty-one years of deceit, trauma, being silenced and gas-lighted, the absence of a loving Mother/Grandmother, abusive/unloving replacements, emotional and psychological abuse.

The fact that the father I love and trusted is capable of such a heart wrenchingly selfish, brutal and misogynist act – she's no longer any use to you, a hinderance with no value, you can coldly dispose of her in such utter disrespect ... this has affected my trust in men and subconsciously, every relationship I've had.

For many years I worked through abandonment issues, believing that our beautiful Mother left of her own accord and had I believed what you said, because she didn't love us anymore. Most, if not every day, I feel the absence of her from our lives.

I have, what I believe are glimpses of memories from that nightmare night. Unfortunately, as a result of the trauma experienced, my defence mechanisms have erased all happy memories of my Mother as well. All of these years, there were always parts of me looking for her, in communes, consulting psychics, registering with The Salvation Army. Haunted by regular thoughts of, 'Why did she leave, where is she, if/when she'll return …?!'

Until the day I realised she wasn't going to. The massive grief of that, on every level.

No Mother to cuddle me when I'm hurt or sad.

No Mother to love, help or advise me.

No Mother to be a role model for my own Mothering.

No weekly home-cooked meals to return home to, no family gatherings, birthdays, Christmas to look forward to.

You took that away and so much more and you had NO RIGHT to. YOU ARE NOT GOD.

There is NO replacement for a loving Mother, especially one who was ill-equipped and not wanting to take on such a role, who rejected us harshly and didn't nurture and love us as we needed and deserved … the absence of these basic human needs has affected my development, attachment, growth and stability. The rejection we suffered by multiple

Mothers (seemingly), affected my self-esteem for many years.

Once I came into the remembrance that it was you who removed her from our lives, my whole world shattered. I wasn't able to complete basic tasks such as grocery shopping, feeding myself properly or socialising. I was working full time at the time, but haven't been able to since, nor have I been able to complete the two university degrees I have begun, despite getting excellent grades. Yes, I made my choices in this, but I now understand the effect this trauma has had on so many aspects of my life.

I didn't confront you right away and the burdens lay heavily on my shoulders. I knew I would be losing my family, my sister in particular, and I didn't think that was fair that I was suffering so much for what YOU'D done. I didn't do anything wrong and yet I was losing so much. Every time I saw you, I was thrown into a trauma response and became extremely emotional and dysfunctional for days afterward. I kept trying to figure out how I would approach the situation, trying to choose the gentlest way for myself and all involved. I didn't want to be the one to bring a tidal wave to the family.

I was diagnosed with PTSD and these symptoms include anxiety and depression, as well as being in a fairly regular state of fight, flight or freeze, of hyper-vigilance and chronic stress. My nervous system is depleted and this affects my general wellbeing, health, energy-levels, happiness, joy and ability to function often at basic tasks, work and relationships at every level. I also developed adult asthma as a result of chronic stress, caused by you. All of this has affected my mothering and ability to be truly present and joyous for my child. She's seen me cry a lot.

Our lives always on hold – at first, always wondering. Secondly, mass media attention, arrest, court dates, appeals and delays ... life on hold, hard to relate or focus on much else of any significance (other than my child, obviously). Nine weeks of intense trial days, more life consumed by grief and anger ... again life, mothering, friendships on hold. Precious time wasted in conversations I don't want to have. Tired of sadness.

The stress of having to hear more and more lies. The grief of losing trust in people who I once believed and now see through their lies, because of your actions.

Waiting, waiting for the verdict. Life on hold again, stress levels and grief heightened.

I went to great lengths to keep your act a secret from my daughter, waiting until she was older to tell her the horrible reality. Unfortunately, her friend told her and I had to explain to my beautiful, innocent daughter why her grandfather killed her Grandmother. She had many questions and anger, confusion, grief. She kept asking me, 'But WHY did he do that?!' The same question that's tortured me over and over now for many years.

Why didn't you just divorce her, let those who love and needed her keep her?!!!! Because of money, for God's sake?!!!! The way you made her invisible, didn't keep her memory alive for her children, rarely spoke of her and when you did, it was with disdain or disrespect ... we had no photos out, no mention of her birthday or what she was like, beautiful moments of her loving us, of her caring & giving heart, her beautiful free spirit ... this has been a massive, gaping lacking hole in my world. Partly filled in by others, but not by you.

As a direct result of your actions, I've lost not only my adoring, kind, wonderful and beautiful Mother, but I've lost my father too. I've lost the sense of protection you were supposed to provide, I've lost at times, the belief that there are good men in the world. It has had a significant impact on my psychological and emotional wellbeing and trying to integrate how on earth the father I love and trusted is capable of such a horrific act of violence against a woman he once supposedly loved, the Mother of his children.

I've also lost my sister, other siblings, cousins and my beautiful nieces.

I lost any remnants of belonging to that immediate family since I came into the remembering that it was you who murdered my Mother.

My daughter doesn't have her loving Grandmother in her life to care for, support and guide her. She's also lost aunties, uncles, cousins … and you, her grandfather.

I have happy memories of your parents … of our Friday family dinners, their attendance at netball games and sports carnivals, occasional babysitting, of cousin holidays with them. You've taken that away from your grandchildren.

I don't have the loving presence of a Grandmother for my child, her practical and emotional support and reprieve from the constant demands of single Mothering. This has taken a massive toll on my health and wellbeing. I've wasted countless and precious hours in counselling and therapy, when I'd rather be playing with my daughter and enjoying life.

As a result of YOUR actions, my wonderful Nanna Simms, while overjoyed to see us, always felt simultaneously deep sorrow when she saw us (or likely often) and I felt somehow responsible for that. I wanted to make it all okay that her beautiful daughter wasn't with us anymore. We would pray, rub Buddha's belly and cry together for her return. As a result of YOUR actions, my Mother's parents chose not to leave her share of inheritance to us (for fear you'd get it, I'm assuming) ... I've also lost your and my Mother's share of your/her home.

Your lies messed me up. The crazy, warped haze inside my brain of trying to make sense of what's right and wrong. Of wanting to believe what I'm told, while the truth screamed at me from the inner knowing of my body, my hidden memories. When I'm being lied to and manipulated by others, it's a familiar and subconsciously sought feeling called trauma bonding. When that's the foundation that's been laid, it affects your whole life until it can be re-programmed and healed. I moved interstate, because the anxiety of potentially running into you on the Sunshine Coast was giving me panic attacks.

It hurts me deeply to think of you in jail, for the rest of your life. But I also choose not to carry your burdens anymore. I need my life back. My daughter needs me back and not overwhelmed by grief anymore. This is how I will honour my beautiful Mother.

The torture of not knowing what happened, or what you did with her body, please tell us where she is.

I hope you will finally admit the truth to yourself and give us the last bit of closure we need, to make at least partial peace with this horrible tragedy.

Once I was finished, I couldn't bear to look at my father anymore, or to be in the same, stifling concrete room as him, void of real air and windows. I went straight to the Botanical Gardens to get barefoot on the earth and comforted by the trees. I was so grateful for my wonderful support, my dear friend Sally and wonderful Trish, from Victim Support Services. Also, for my lovely friends for watching my daughter so I could go into this situation feeling more resourced, grounded and able to meet my own needs. I was dysfunctional for weeks after giving my victim impact statement.

I have long felt an urgent and burning need to find my Mother's remains – and although I do believe there are at least two people who know what happened to my Mother and it's possible we may come to learn the whole truth – the dire urgency I once felt has significantly subsided since my father's trial. I don't think I've given up hope; sometimes hope is all I have.

After my father was found guilty and before he was sentenced, 'Lyn's Law' was passed in the New South Wales parliament. The rule means 'no body, no parole', and it makes it impossible for offenders who wilfully and deliberately refuse to disclose information about their victims' remains to be granted parole. If my father doesn't reveal where my Mother is, he will not be eligible for parole.

On the 1ˢᵗ of December 2022, my father was sentenced to twenty-four years in jail. It is heartbreaking for me to know he will likely die behind bars.

In his sentencing, Justice Harrison said the sentence should reflect the 'disapprobation with which his self-indulgent brutality must be viewed by Australian society'.

'Mr Dawson planned to kill his wife. Whatever means Mr Dawson employed to kill her, he intended that result. He did so in a domestic context and in her own home,' Justice Harrison continued.

'Mr Dawson must be taken to have known and appreciated the injury, emotional harm and loss that his actions were likely to cause to Lynette Dawson's daughters and her other relatives,' he added. 'Tragically her death deprived her young daughters of their mother so that a significant part of the harm caused to others, and by inference to the community, as a consequence of her death, is the sad fact that Lynette Dawson was treated by her husband, the father of the very same girls, as completely dispensable.'

I didn't rejoice when the sentence was handed down. I was consumed with a heavy sadness. I accepted the trial and sentencing as a necessary part of the process, and I'm glad at least part of the truth has been told – that my Mother didn't abandon us – but I still wish the whole situation never happened at all (obviously!). I believe there's more to the story and wonder if we'll ever know the whole truth.

Whilst I was in Sydney to do a second interview with *60 Minutes*, I met up with my Mother's friend Anna, who was a big part of *The Teacher's Pet* podcast. Anna is a beautiful Italian woman who has a lot of love for my Mum. She shared that love with me and my daughter, telling Kialah to call her 'Nonna'. I went for a walk with Anna on the bush trails at Bayview behind where we used to live. It might sound delusional, but we were looking for my Mother's remains. Both Anna and I were drawn to a particular spot. We sat down on some rocks there and Anna spoke about my Mum. She told me she dreams about my Mother often. She feels a lot of regret. 'I wish I would have done more. Why didn't we? Why didn't I?' she kept saying. Above the rock we sat beneath, off the trail in the bush, I found a Mother of Mary statue. We both thought it was a sign. We didn't find anything else that day.

I also met up with some of my Mother's family on her birthday, September the 25th, at Long Reef again. I was grateful to Uncle Greg and Auntie Merilyn for watching Kialah whilst I was being interviewed and it was lovely for Kialah to feel the presence of loving family, to partly fill the huge, lacking void.

A Diary Entry

3rd of December 2022
Northern New South Wales

I'm feeling really depressed today. Some days I can put the heaviness to the side but today it sits on my head and chest like lead weights in a thick, dense fog that can't find the light, but I know it's there and it will come again.

There isn't a corner of my life that hasn't been touched by the loss of my Mother. Some days, I feel like I'm in the path of a landslide as the rocks pile down on top of me, crushing me, suffocating me.

It's not just birthdays, Christmas, Mother's Day or the 8th of January that trigger grief for me around my Mother. It's every time I see a loving mother/child relationship, every time one of my friends posts on social media stating how much they love their amazing mum. I know I'm not the only person in the world who misses their mum. And I realise not everybody who has one has a loving and nurturing relationship with them.

In some ways, I've adapted to the reality of not having a mother, but in multiple and vast ways, I have not. Her absence weaves in my every day and lingers in conversations when people absent-mindedly state, 'Oh, you know how it is', in regards to a mother or family experience. It's not that person's fault, but internally I'm screaming and crying, 'No, I don't fucking know what it's like.' But on the outside,

I give a half smile, usually waiting for them to realise their insensitivity. Most times, they don't.

How it feels to move through this world without that solid person who has your back and loves you unconditionally — only others who don't have that can comprehend the magnitude of it.

In 2023, as I was working on this manuscript, my father returned to court to face a second trial where he was accused of having a sexual relationship with an underage student; the student he would go on to marry. I wasn't given a heads-up about the case and found out through a text message. I purposely did not follow the trial closely. I couldn't put myself through it all again. I didn't have the energy, time, mental health or capacity to. I was already running at a deficit. It wasn't a choice; it was a matter of survival.

When my father was found guilty of carnal knowledge in June, old wounds were reopened. Judge Sarah Huggett convicted my father, officially making him both a killer and a sexual predator. The judge found that my father went to the Time and Tide Hotel in Cromer, where students and teachers would mingle on Friday nights, because dad was 'interested and attracted to the complainant'.

My father listened to the judge's ruling via a video link from Long Bay Correctional Complex, where he is imprisoned. The evidence was damning: he had held hands with his student lover in the schoolyard, canoodled with her in his school office and dropped love notes into her backpack. On her Year 11 report card, my father wrote that the student was 'a pleasure to teach'. The schoolgirl told the court she'd been 'groomed' in the playground. She said my father took her to his parents' house while they were away, where they engaged in sexual activities on their bed. 'I was told to keep it a secret,' the student said.

It's not a secret anymore. The trial has put a spotlight on the inappropriate and predatory behaviour by some teachers who worked on the Northern Beaches of Sydney in the 1980s. The verdict has paved the way for other cases to be brought to the court. Since reading the evidence, I've always known that there was more to my father's story; that the depravity ran deeper than just him. This might be the tip of the iceberg, which is a terrifying and sickening thought.

After the judge handed down her guilty verdict and left the courtroom, my father muttered to himself. 'Fuck, fuck, fuck,' he said.

Sometimes there are no other words.

CHAPTER FIFTEEN

Ocean Lullabies and Invisible Arms That Hold

If I was to express the anger and rage I feel internally, it would be akin to the Goddess Kali, the Goddess of Death and Rebirth. Do you know her? She's the one with many arms holding heads, with a tongue sticking out, looking fierce. She is revered or feared – and often misunderstood, in my opinion. The destruction she brings is necessary to clear away the unwanted debris. I'm aware our society doesn't know how to hold space for that amount of anger and rage, so I shove it back down, where it burns a hole in my solar plexus, just waiting for a healthy channel. And I'm hopeful this book is one of them.

My anger and rage are greater than just my own. Yes, it's toward my father and his removal of my Mother. But it's also toward the misogynistic patriarchy and the removal of the mother from religion, Western culture in general and so many of our practices. Ever since I was young, the Father, the Son and the Holy Spirit just seemed to be missing half of the equation. Although I could feel some beauty and comfort there, I wondered: what about the Mother, the Daughter and their Holy Spirit? Our patriarchal society isn't working. There are unnecessary wars, family domestic violence and sexual abuse is at epic volatile proportions, ancient forests are being mass cleared to build roads, areas of cultural significance are decimated to build mines, where we rape the Earth, kill many creatures and leave the surrounding areas polluted and dead, our penal system has a high rate of repeat offenders, so one might question the effectiveness of that system. The list goes on and on ... Equal pay still isn't happening; also women pay a luxury tax on necessary sanitary items – though at least fifty-one per cent of the population would likely agree it's not a luxury – while Viagra is government subsidised. And then there's the pink tax, where the same products with the same ingredients made by the same company, cost significantly more when they're marketed for women than the same product intended for men. What the hell!? If women were adequately represented in all areas of government, and the patriarchal mindset were to take its rightful place in the past, this would never happen.

I find the inequality of it all infuriating. Maybe it's because of the injustice I've experienced in my life, but I feel particularly sensitive to the harshness of the world. I don't have any tolerance for it.

After my father's murder trial, I felt – and looked – like I'd aged twenty years in only four. I didn't really care, though, as I think grey hairs and wrinkles are beautiful. It has never made any sense to me, the narrow definition of beauty our society ascribes to, pertaining to youth only. It greatly saddens me to see people pumping their faces and bodies full of toxic shit to obtain a supposedly accepted level of 'beauty'. I find it so strange, how people find 'faults' in the natural ageing processes and feel a need to cover their 'flaws' with make-up. Why is it, that only women (and those identifying as female and non-binary) wear make-up? If women want to wear make-up for themselves, that's fine, do what you want, but I find it sad when women feel the need to do it for other people or especially for a society that has its priorities in completely false paradigms. Unnatural and unachievable concepts of superficial beauty are harmful to us all. They enable men like my father, who feel their wives have 'let themselves go' to trade them in so callously for a newer model. Women are not cars. We are not possessions. We don't belong to you. Women do not lose value – or beauty – as we age, we gain it.

Around the time of my Mother's birthday in 2019, I began the process of creating a not-for-profit to honour my Mum, the Lynette Joy Foundation. It has been a slow birthing process, as I haven't had any excess energy to offer as yet, but the dreaming phase is evolving and taking shape into a more solid form as I complete my book. I have many visions of what I would like to do, including education in high schools regarding healthy relationships, identifying red flags, as well as support for those at risk as a result of coming from families with domestic violence. When I lived in Hawaii, I volunteered in a program called 'Challenge Day'. It was geared at bullying in schools as well as helping create compassion and empathy. It was massively profound and though I wasn't there long enough to see long-term results, the results I did see over just three days were remarkable. The program left me feeling inspired and hopeful, and I would love to be involved in bringing elements of the program into the schools in Australia to help prevent abusive relationships from forming and being entered into, as it can be very difficult and dangerous to get out once you're in them. There are other amazing programs being offered in Australia, such as 'Tomorrow Man'. One of their goals is to 'Re-invent Masculinity', and they run education programs to encourage young men to identify, feel and talk about their emotions and support each other in doing that. I cry with inspiration every time I read their posts. Although not specifically for DV – their goal is to prevent suicide – it is directly related, and I feel their achievements are an excellent preventative and effective tool to aid a culture shift.

That's what we desperately need: a culture shift. Even if someone doesn't have a history of violence, that doesn't mean they're not capable of it. Just because he doesn't hit you, doesn't mean he's not abusive. Abuse often starts with control. It starts with criticising how you look or what you wear, controlling where you go and who you see, isolating you from family and friends, and limiting your access to money and support.

It is hard to know where to begin to create change and an understanding is certainly needed that DV goes beyond the individual's and family circumstances, that there are numerous cultural and socio/political factors involved. We need to get to the root of the problem and disassemble these unhealthy paradigms between misused power and vulnerability and learn to recognise when they're unsafe and destructive.

Domestic violence needs to be stopped before it starts. It is my hope that with this book, and the Lynette Joy Foundation, I will play my part in helping to make at least some small difference in the world. May my Mother's death give others in her situation the strength to leave. I pray they will have support to do so safely. I hope to remind victim/survivors they're not alone.

My anger is bigger than me, and I hope that I can channel it toward making real change. I'm not afraid of my anger, but I don't want to be consumed nor held back by it. I don't know if I'll ever be completely free of it, so I'm choosing to harness it.

The Goddess Kali is both frightening and awe-inspiring. She isn't afraid of her force. She is the quintessential embodiment of shakti, female power, and she represents the ultimate goal of feminism – for women to be free, no longer oppressed or inferior. She commands respect and settles for no less.

I realise it's necessary to accept the truth of my situation, but it has been a massive process to arrive at this point. When I think about my dad in jail, it breaks my heart, even though he's caused a lot of unnecessary pain and anguish as a result of his selfish actions. I know a lot of people think he should rot in hell, that he's getting what he deserves, and I understand why people feel like that. I don't claim to have the answers, but I don't believe that the current justice system is working effectively from a societal perspective. It is my belief that demonising abusers won't fix the root of the problem; nor will they feel safe to ask for help when they're steeped in shame, hatred from others and self-loathing.

Those who've committed crimes, and who are capable of remorse, need support to understand their behaviour and to find a better way of existing in the world. I don't necessarily think putting them in jail and causing them to suffer further is the way to do that. Jail reinforces the fight or flight survival mode that many have been born or forced into and keeps these people stuck in those patterns; that doesn't bode well for rehabilitation and improved life choices. Some people do their time and come out with a renewed vision and a plan to turn their life around, while others are not capable of rehabilitation at all. Restorative Justice is an amazing process for fostering mutual dialogue and healing because it utilises the qualities of empathy and compassion and creates a circle of healing in a majority of cases where the process is engaged. I'd love to see Restorative Justice become more common practice. In my dad's case, I don't think it's possible because he's still in denial about what he's done.

My hope for my father is that his time in jail will allow him to become more honest with himself. I want him to process things and take responsibility for them, to admit what he did to my Mother, feel regretful, and tell us where she is. I hope that before he dies, he can reach a place of forgiveness within himself for what he's done. I don't know if he's capable of these things, but this is my hope.

A Dream

1st of March 2023
Northern New South Wales

I'm in jail. There's a casual, friendly vibe. A bunch of people have escaped, so the guards are chasing them, leaving the jail unattended. I go to where the keys are kept in a safe box on the wall and retrieve a bunch of them, hoping to find the right one before they return. I pass the window and a beautiful man on the outside sees me, the same one I've seen before with olive skin, green eyes and curly, golden brown hair. He turns and stares at me as though slightly amused, or as if he recognises me.

I quickly look away, not wanting to be seen or recognised as I escape.

I'm genuinely grateful to all of the people over the years who have taken their precious time and care to reach out to me with their empathy, compassion and well wishes. I understand it's natural for those of us who are essentially kind to want to ease and eradicate the suffering they see in the world. In that, there's something so intricately beautiful in the way our experiences and care weaves us together and binds us in human interconnectedness. Additionally, we might admire strength and determination in another, and feel inspired by their ability to overcome adverse situations. I don't intend to infringe upon or lay claim to knowing anyone else's truth by stating this truth of mine, but I can honestly say that as much as I resist, distract myself and get bogged at times in the suffering when I'm *in* it, it has also been my most expansive teacher. I've grown in my awareness, my ability to identify my own needs and truths, to develop skills of holding space for myself and others, and to deepen in my capacity for compassion. I have, in the absence of a Mother, turned to Mother Earth for nurturing and soothing. I am grateful for the deep and alchemical connection I feel with this amazing planet, surrounding us with beauty and firmly holding our feet. I have journeyed through my absolute anguish and despair in cycles, and each time found solace upon returning home to centre, an alignment with a Source of love, greater than myself.

As my favourite poet, Kahlil Gibran (*The Prophet*) states so beautifully …

Joy and Sorrow

Then a woman said, Speak to us of Joy and Sorrow.

And he answered:

Your joy is your sorrow unmasked.

And your selfsame well from which your laughter rises was oftentimes filled with your tears.

And how else can it be?

The deeper that sorrow carves into your being, the more joy you can contain.

Is not the cup that holds your wine the very cup that was burned in the potter's oven? And is not the lute that soothes your spirit the very wood that was hollowed with knives? When you are joyous, look deep into your heart and you shall find it is only that which has given you sorrow that is giving you joy.

When you are sorrowful, look again in your heart, and you shall see that in truth you are weeping for that which has been your delight.

Some of you say, 'Joy is greater than sorrow,' and others say, 'Nay, sorrow is the greater.'

But I say unto you, they are inseparable.

Together they come, and when one sits alone with you at your board, remember that the other is asleep upon your bed.

Verily you are suspended like scales between your sorrow and your joy. Only when you are empty are you at standstill and balanced.

When the treasure-keeper lifts you to weigh his gold and his silver, needs must your joy or your sorrow rise or fall.

I haven't felt unbounded joy, with the lightness of laughter that rings like a bell, since remembering it was my dad who took my Mother away. My Mother's name, Lynette Joy, is a reminder to me that joy is something to reclaim through all of this. This is the most profound way I can honour her now. My Mother's story lives on in me; it permeates into everyday reality and is woven through every fibre of my being. I've tried to put my sorrow aside and 'get on with my life', but it wasn't done yet. My hope is that by telling my story, getting it outside of my inner world and into the outer world, it will no longer have such a strong hold on almost every aspect of my life. That instead of crying when I see photos of my beautiful Mother, I can smile and feel the love as equally as the loss. I am not only reclaiming my Mother's story and my story as our own, I'm moving these chapters further into the past and writing new ones. New chapters that re-wire the occasions that have been saturated by grief, so they can now become a celebration with my beautiful daughter as we dissolve the ancestral trauma, to rebirth a new dawn and brighter day.

When I asked my daughter if she had anything she'd like to say about her Nanna Lyn, this is what she told me …

Hi special grandma in heaven, I always see you as a butterfly and every time I do, I send my love.

You would be so proud of me, grandma, and you're probably right here with me now.

Love you.

Most of the Dawsons have now disowned and ostracised me. The Dawson DNA dominantly carries the genetics of brown hair and eyes. My Mother's family are fair and blue-eyed. I was the only cousin on the Dawson side with fair hair and blue eyes and I always loved that I inherited my Mother's genes and share my Mother's blue eyes. I felt that bonded her and I, as I carry these codes of hers inside myself, but also in existence beyond time and space.

When I close my eyes, I can see my Mother smiling with her sparkling blue eyes. I carry her gently in my heart, always. I know my Mother is so much more than this tragic story that she's now come to be known by. As we embrace and integrate the shadows cast by such devastation, I feel her graceful essence and playful spirit weaving and dancing through me. I feel her blessings shining on my daughter and I, loving us always. When I would more achingly miss her, it was to the ocean I would go to be comforted and nourished. Ocean lullabies and invisible arms that hold me are what has carried me through these immensely challenging times. And when I gaze at the aquatic, sparkly blue waters and the vast blue sky, I am reminded of my Mother's Eyes, sparkling with love.

This is a photo of the Mother Mary statue I
found off the trail in the bush at Bayview, while
I was looking for my Mother's remains with
her friend Anna. Is it a sign of something?
We felt it was.

Resources

If you or someone you know is in immediate danger, call 000 in Australia or 111 in New Zealand immediately.

The following services can put you in touch with the best service for your needs.

1800RESPECT

This national family violence and sexual assault counselling service is available 24 hours a day, 7 days a week. It's confidential and free to call. They can also help with advice about online safety if you think someone is watching your online activities.

To contact 1800RESPECT:

- call **1800 737 732** to speak with a professional counsellor
- use the services directory on the **1800RESPECT** website to find help in your area:
  https://www.1800respect.org.au/services/search
- go to the **1800RESPECT** website:
  https://www.1800respect.org.au/

1800 ELDERHelp line

The Elder Abuse Help Line directs you to your state or territory service. Operating hours vary. Call 1800 353 374.

Black Rainbow

Black Rainbow (https://blackrainbow.org.au/) is a national organisation for promoting the health and wellbeing of Aboriginal and Torres Strait Islander LGBTI+ people. They provide information, as well as a pre-paid phone and data credit service for Aboriginal and Torres Strait Islander LGBTI+ people affected by family and domestic violence.

Compass

Compass (https://www.compass.info/) is a national website with information and resources about the abuse of older Australians. If you or an older person you know needs help, you can use it to find support in your area.

Disability Gateway

The Disability Gateway connects you to information about family and domestic violence and support services in your state or territory. You can find this information in the Safety and Help section of the Disability Gateway website: https://www.disabilitygateway.gov.au/safety-help

Family Relationship Advice

The Family Relationship Advice Line can help you with family issues and separation. They can also refer you to local services for more help.

Call them on **1800 050 321**. The line is open:
- Monday to Friday, 8 am to 8 pm
- Saturday, 10 am to 4 pm.

Read more about the Family Relationship Advice Line on the Family Relationships website: https://www.familyrelationships.gov.au/talk-someone/advice-line

Intellectual Disability Rights Service

The Intellectual disability rights service is a disability advocacy service and a community legal centre. They help people with disability to promote and protect their rights. To contact them, you can either:

- call **02 9318 0144**
- go to the Intellectual Disability Rights service website: http://www.idrs.org.au/

Kids Helpline

Kids Helpline is a free service for young people aged 5 to 25.
To contact them:

- call **1800 551 800** at any time
- go to the Kids Helpline website: https://www.kidshelpline.com.au/.

Lifeline

Lifeline offers personal crisis support services if you're affected by family and domestic violence.

Call them on **131 114** at any time.

Read more on the Lifeline website: https://www.lifeline.org.au/get-help/information-and-support/domestic-and-family-violence

MensLine Australia

MensLine Australia is a phone and online support service. They provide specialist help to people affected by family and domestic violence. They also offer support to people using violence.

To contact them:

- call **1300 789 978** at any time
- go to the MensLine Australia website: http://www.mensline.org.au/

Men's Referral Service
The Men's Referral Service is a free phone counselling, information and referral service. They help men to stop using violence and abuse against family members.
    To contact them:
* call **1300 766 491**
* go to the No to Violence website: https://www.ntv.org.au/
The line is open 24 hours a day, 7 days a week and is available nationally.

National Legal Aid
National Legal Aid can help you find the legal aid commission in your state or territory. Read more about their services on the National legal aid website: https://www.nationallegalaid.org/

QLife
QLife provides anonymous support and referrals for LGBTI+ people who may be experiencing family and domestic violence.
    To contact them:
* call **1800 184 527**
* go to the QLife website to chat online: https://qlife.org.au/
The phone line and webchat are available from 3 pm to midnight, every day.

Raising children
The Raising Children Network website has a list of helplines and other resources for children experiencing abuse: https://raisingchildren.net.au/grown-ups/services-support/services-families/child-sexual-abuse-helplines-and-services

Say It Out Loud
Say It Out Loud provides information on family and domestic violence, safety planning and referral services for LGBTI+ people. It is a national resource, and also provides information on state and territory specific supports: https://sayitoutloud.org.au/

Women's Legal Services Australia
www.wlsa.org.au
Their mission is to promote a legal system that is safe, supportive, non-discriminatory and responsive to the needs of women

Ask Izzy
Ask Izzy is a free and anonymous website to find national and local support. It includes services like housing, meals, healthcare, counselling, legal advice and many more: https://askizzy.org.au/

Daisy
Daisy is a free app developed by 1800RESPECT that connects you to services in your local area. You can create a list of services and save them. This includes legal, housing, financial and children's services. You can also search the internet with Daisy and understand what to expect when contacting a service.

Download Daisy from Google Play or the App Store.

Sunny
Sunny is a free app developed by 1800RESPECT and women with disability. Sunny supports all women with disability impacted by sexual assault and family and domestic violence.

Sunny helps you to:
- understand what violence and abuse are
- learn about different types of violence
- understand what has happened
- know your rights
- find people who can help.

Download Sunny from Google Play or the App Store.

Gathered under a giant fig tree during a
Day of the Dead ceremony that honours loved
ones. Auntie Merilyn, Uncle Greg, me and
Auntie Pat remembered and paid tribute to
their beloved sister, my beautiful Mother.

Acknowledgements

I give most extensive gratitude to our Mother Earth, giver and sustainer of life, in particular to the divine lands upon which I reside. Most importantly, to the original and ongoing custodians, the people of the Bundjalung Nation. To every piece of dirt, rock and sand I've ever set foot upon, the healing of your nature soothes and inspires my writing and peace. Vanessa Radnidge, my publisher: you are and have been completely amazing and a lovely support, thanks so much for seeing this story before you knew I was writing one, for reaching out and giving me this opportunity to reclaim my story. This book certainly couldn't have come to fruition in this capacity without my co-writer, Alley Pascoe. You trudged through the factual and linear details that my brain and heart couldn't be tortured with anymore. You took my creative chaos and helped assemble it into order, your enthusiasm and encouragement lit the way through some dark tunnels when I was drowning in my grief … you were my ally and sanity weaver, thank you, Alley.

Beautiful friend Tegan, your grounded and ever-present support of Kialah has been vital and appreciated at every level. I can relax in full trust when she's in your loving care and that has allowed me to expand more fully into the book-writing process. The Hachette production team is a well-oiled machine with competent and wonderful people contributing their expertise to aid in this creation. There's a lot more that goes on behind the scenes and I thank you all wholeheartedly for your caring contributions: Emma Rafferty, Fiona Hazard, Louise Stark, Lillian Kovats, Alysha Farry, Kate Taperell, Alexa Roberts, Isabel Staas, Caitlin Murphy, Chris Sims, Kelly Gaudry, Catriona Feeney, Giovanna Nunziato and the whole team. Thank you to Christa Moffitt and Graeme Jones.

Thank you also to Hedley Thomas for your ongoing support and encouragement.

My sincere gratitude to psychic mediums Teena Angelia and Michelle R Price The Lightworker in giving generously of your time to help me locate my Mum's body.

So much love to Stephy, Mikey, Hayley and Lesley for pulling together at a crucial time, to give me necessary respite from mothering and extra time for my writing. Our friends Jan and Colin, our adopted 'Grandparents', thank you so much for your care, time with and embracing of Kialah, I'm so grateful we found each other. The wonderful Sjhara and Shaa at Sacred Earth Medicine, your intuition and generous donation of Ceremonial Cacao helped me immensely in my writing process. I was able to move through some blocks to access that which had been previously inaccessible, as Mama Cacao brought the sweet relief of clarity whilst activating my heart. Huge thanks to all of the friends and even some I'm yet to meet, who extend queries into my and my daughter's wellbeing and progress of my book. Acknowledgements to my journals throughout the years, my most beloved therapist, dream and record keepers ... this book could not have been written without you.

Obviously my biggest gratitude to my beautiful Mother, who gave me life, a solid foundation of Love and nurturing for the first four-and-a-half years of my life. I'm certain you've been with me whilst I write and possibly even whispered in my ear. I hope I've honoured you well and reclaimed our story in the best possible way.

hachette
AUSTRALIA

If you would like to find out more about
Hachette Australia, our authors, upcoming events
and new releases, you can visit our website or our
social media channels:

hachette.com.au
HachetteAustralia
HachetteAus